ESSENTIAL MONEY
GUIDEBOOK
Simple and Sustainable
Personal Finance for Real People

Wes Karchut, M.B.A.

Darby Karchut, M.Ed.

 Copper Square Studios

Essential Money Guidebook: Simple and Sustainable
Personal Finance for Real People
Copyright © 2013 Wes Karchut and Darby Karchut
Published by Copper Square Studios
Colorado Springs, CO
ISBN 978-0-9741145-1-4
Library of Congress Control Number 2014903315

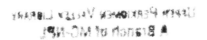

Acknowledgments

The authors wish to acknowledge the following organizations, government resources and individuals for their invaluable assistance in the preparation of this book.

Fair Isaac and Company
Bank of America
Charles Schwab
Federal Deposit Insurance Coverage
Federal Housing Authority
Bankrate.com
Federal Reserve Board of Governors
United States Department of Education
United States Department of the Treasury
Federal Deposit Insurance Coverage
H&R Block
Federal Trade Commission

Contents

11   Invest Like the Pros   162

Final Thoughts   182

Appendix A   Compound Interest   184

Why You Should Read This Book

Personal finance books would rather not tell you this:

1. Complicated financial plans and tedious budgets are doomed to failure.

2. Few people want to become financial experts. In fact, managing their own money is a bit scary.

3. Life is just more fun when you don't have to ride herd on every dollar you spend.

The goal of this book is to spare you from the tedium of money management boot camps and makeovers. If instead, you make the right financial moves at the right time, your results will far exceed any of those possible from the penny-pinching chores that typically pass for sound financial advice.

If you could care less about personal finance, but you also acknowledge that you need to know a little something about it, then this book is for you. Maybe, you've just started a family, and you feel a heightened sense of responsibility toward your spouse and children. Or, you've finally found the courage to confront the realities of your retirement. You might be newly single along with all of the financial responsibilities now on your plate. You may even be retired, and you want to make your money last longer. If you find yourself in any of these situations, reading this book will be the best investment you can make for your financial future.

What this book is about

Knowledge Based

You will learn to make better money choices so that you can optimize your personal finances — no matter what your lifestyle choices. There is a tremendous leverage factor when you make the right decision at the right time. Brutal budgeting or financial dieting is no match compared to smart financial decision-making.

Simple

You won't be asked to become a bookkeeping whiz or a half-crazed, recycle-store shopper. Nor will you be asked to master the intricacies of compound interest or collateral loan terms.

Nonjudgmental

Nowhere will you be asked to live in a in a particular way. There is no best way, only the way that makes your life most fulfilling for you.

Sustainable

This is not a quick fix book. In fact, it is just the opposite. The more quickly and radically you make changes, the less likely they will last. You won't find any 30-day programs inside.

Balanced

Balanced means that there is an acceptable trade-off between reward and sacrifice, shared equally among all family members. Notice that this book does not promise a life free of sacrifice, only that it be commensurate with reward and contribution.

Fulfilling

This book is written in the belief that while any of us can
be victims in the short term, in the long term we are free to
choose otherwise. You may not deserve your current circumstance, but in the long term, you do. That is your choice. If
you feel that you can have a better future, a more fulfilling
life, then this book is for you.

Money management skills

Along with learning some fundamentals of personal finance,
you will also gain critical, twenty-first century money
management skills. Once again, ninety percent of what
you learn will improve your financial situation without any
lifestyle changes, and without regard to your current financial
condition (unless you're bankrupt, in which case you should
find a good attorney).

Here are a few of the financial concepts you will learn.

1. Recognizing and avoiding spending traps
2. Stopping identity theft cold
3. Avoiding financial catastrophes
4. Becoming credit score savvy
5. Taming student loans — yours or your childrens
6. Protecting yourself from financial scams
7. Getting the most from your retirement income without
   running out of money
8. Avoiding mental traps that handicap your wealth
9. Getting a handle on your finances in less in fifteen
   minutes

10. Preventing a financial meltdown or future home foreclosure

11. Protecting your credit

12. Improving your credit score

13. Buying and refinancing your home the smart way

14. Making compound interest work for you

15. Creating a simple money management plan

16. Investing the smart way

17. Getting the most from your Social Security

18. Setting an achievable retirement savings goal

19. Eliminating dumb spending habits

20. Unlocking the power of your net worth

Much of what you will find in reading this book is about replacing wealth-killing, dumb decisions with savvy, wealth-building money moves. Armed with this information, you will know what to do and when, without agonizing over spreadsheets or putting yourself on a painful financial diet.

Money and Teens: Savvy Money Skills

If you are a financial newbie or just want a primer on the basics of finance, our book: *Money and Teens: Savvy Money Skills* is a good companion text. Don't let the name fool you. It is written for young adults, but as the winner of the *2013 Book of the Year EIFLE Award* for excellence in financial literacy education, the information it contains exceeds much of what many adults will ever learn about personal finance. Some of this information has proven so valuable that a number of the topics have been expanded upon in this book.

It's not about working hard

Successfully managing your money shouldn't be another job. There's a popular, stock-picking TV commentator who advises viewers to do at least one hour of homework a week for every investment they make. Yuck. Who wants to do that? Most likely, reading one book on personal finance will be the most effort you'll ever want to put into your finances.

If you have better things to do than manage your money, then invest a little time now, and own your financial future.

What this book is not about

Essential Money Guidebook is not a 30-day fix-it program — a boot camp designed to help you whip your finances into shape. Money management is no different than any other craft, like carpentry or sewing. You have to know something about your tools along with how to use them, before you can do anything useful. You wouldn't build a house without knowing how to use a saw and a level, or sew a dress lacking the skills to use a needle and thread.

This is not a book full of tips, tricks, and techniques, which are fine as far as they go, but without some framework of understanding, you cannot hope to apply that knowledge effectively. It's like teaching someone ten ways to remove a gallbladder, and then expecting them to become a surgeon. In a similar vein, you have to learn the fundamentals of money management (with some advanced concepts as well), so that you can adapt to changes in your personal situation or the broader economy.

Reading *Essential Money Guidebook* will not make you rich, nor bring you effortless wealth. Anyone over the age of twelve knows better than that, or should. Authors who make those promises are only out to bring wealth to themselves by selling you their book. If you live beyond your means, no book can help you stay afloat.

This book will not ask you to disrupt your lifestyle in order to put your finances on the straight and narrow. Whatever changes you do make, if any, will be small, simple, and rewarding. In fact, ninety percent of what you will learn from this book can be applied without any change to your lifestyle whatsoever.

> *This book is about making smart financial decisions,*
> *not about working hard.*

Essential Money Guidebook is intended to work with your lifestyle and not to remake it. Here you will find no judgments or preaching. At the end of the day, personal finance, unsupported by your unique lifestyle choices, will not be sustainable.

> *Your lifestyle choices should be first and foremost, ahead of*
> *managing your money, and not the other way around.*

1   Consumer Savvy

In this chapter you will learn how businesses use the latest psychological marketing strategies to manipulate you into spending more of your money, while discouraging you from shopping their competition. Consistent with the theme of this book, consumer savvy is not a checklist of tips and techniques on how to become a smart consumer (although for those who can't live without a list, there are extensive examples at the end of this chapter). Rather, it gives you real weapons to fight back against consumer traps and tricks.

Psychological warfare

Much has changed in the last twenty years. Whereas manufacturers and service providers used to focus on innovation or improved functionality, they now spend as much effort or more on selling at a deep psychological level.

This psychological warfare against the consumer has been brought about largely by what could best be termed as an over abundance of just about everything. Accelerated product innovation cycles, aided by expanding global trade, lie at the heart of our embarrassment of riches. Foreign trading partners have mastered the art of reverse engineering to create cheaper, look-alike products that hit store shelves practically before the original products. Witness the stunning reversal of fortunes for the Apple iPhone as an example. At one time, for all too brief a time, Apple enjoyed almost total market dominance. Only a few years later, they now find themselves chasing Samsung and losing ground.

Service businesses as well as manufacturing businesses have all experienced this increased level of competition. The last recession unleashed many a hungry manager, with enough contacts and money to set up a competing shop.

Unfortunately, this intense competition hasn't translated into a bonanza for the consumer, owing largely to some of the shrewd ways businesses have learned to market their products. Don't misunderstand, there is real competition and you can take advantage of it, but only if you recognize the game. Once you do, then you are free to play it as well — to your benefit.

Understanding the game

Let's begin with some fundamentals — understanding the motivations of the players, be it Apple, Toyota, a local plumber, or most every other business on the planet. Yes, their motivation is ultimately about making money, but it's lately become more about the way they make their money, and the amount of money that has taken center stage.

The highest aspiration of most every company, despite claims to the contrary, is to become a monopoly, or the sole source from which you can purchase a product or service. The many benefits of having a monopoly include the freedom to raise prices while lowering customer service — think cell phone companies or cable TV.

In pursuit of the goal to become a monopoly, businesses also must avoid too much of a good thing. If a company becomes too dominant in its market, then you can be sure the government will intercede sooner or later. Monopolies like the local utility company, for example, are not the kind of monopolies that businesses strive to become. The trick is to control the market, without attracting attention.

On the other end of the scale are businesses which sell a commodity, again either a product or service. Agricultural products are a good example. One farmer's corn is virtually the same as another. Pricing freedom is pretty much zero.

Every business lies somewhere along the spectrum between a business selling commodities and a monopoly. And these commodity businesses want nothing more than to become a full-on monopoly. There are ways they can do this that are good for you the consumer, such as product and service innovation, and there are other more devious ways — a bit easier to do, unfortunately.

This is the game. Businesses will bust a gut to get away from selling a commodity product or service; in other words, they desperately want to differentiate their product or service from their competitors so that consumers will think there is no competition. Should a business fail to win this game, they pay a very painful, if not lethal, price. A business that can't differentiate its product or service will sooner or later have to admit that fact, and engage in the one thing they hate the most — discounting. And the more they discount, the more they have to discount, because that's all they have to differentiate themselves. It's a race to the bottom. Their ultimate fate is to wind up competing as the lowest-priced bidder.

Just as it is the goal of every business to become a monopoly, it is the goal (or should be) of every consumer to find those businesses that have decided to become the lowest-price bidder. Most every product or service on the planet has at least one such business, and perhaps dozens.

Let's look at how this monopoly quest plays itself out. Now the problem facing a business aspiring to be a monopoly is that the best way, through innovation, is really hard. It takes a lot of money and smarts to make something truly better, especially if it's been around for a while. So, the next best thing is to create a local monopoly, the only car dealership in a small town or the only gas station for the next forty miles, for example.

Those that can't be local monopolies generally settle for becoming what can best be termed 'situational monopolies'. This is the type of monopoly that everyone experiences when they enter the hospital or after they drop their car off for repairs. You may have lots of choices right up to the point you commit, and once you do, you have effectively no choice. Their game is to convince you to trust them, but at the same time share as little consumer information as possible up front as they herd you through the front door — more on this later.

Businesses that can't achieve monopoly status by any other means have yet another card up their sleeves. They can make a fashion statement. Boots are boots as far as functionality goes, and then there are Ugg boots. A Dell computer does everything you ever need a computer to do, but a Mac is more cool. How about coffee? Starbucks. Or a purse? Coach.

The psychological marketing strategy

Finally there remains the trench warfare of commodity businesses — those fighting to climb out of the primordial commodity ooze onto the beach of the monopoly. These are the pest control companies and roofing contractors on the small business end, and the airline and cell phone companies on the large business end.

Enter the psychological marketing strategy, the uppermost goal of which is to convince the customer that a product or service is indeed unique and therefore entitled to greater pricing freedom, along with generally poorer customer service, and maybe an attitude to boot. Many times there is no need to even convince the consumer, there is only the need to wear the consumer out, or to let them fool themselves.

Now, as promised, following is a list, but by no means a complete list, of ways that businesses employ these psychological marketing strategies. Like the spy game, this is a constantly evolving effort. One wonders whether businesses wouldn't be better off if they just spent their money on product innovation, rather than consumer manipulation.

Matching competitor prices

This tactic, usually employed by large retailers like Sears and Home Depot, promises that they will match any price offered by a competitor for the same model, such as a kitchen appliance or big screen TV. The only problem is that the model is unique to each of these retailers. Or rather the model number is unique. You will never find a cheaper price for the exact same model, because no competitor will ever have the exact same model number. End of comparison shopping.

Bundling

Although cable TV has employed this tactic for years, lately everyone is getting into the act, including pest control services and even quick lube and oil businesses. The basic idea is sound in that businesses package together a range of services or products and offer the package for a discount. Over time, however they have determined that it is far more profitable to add more low or no value services as an excuse to pump up the price. The low-price quick lube has evolved into the 20-point engine check with eco-friendly fluid top-offs, and refills. Even such things as bagged salads, with their dozens of odd yet colorful ingredients fall into this category.

Unbundling

The flip side of the bundled or package deal is to unbundle services or products and charge for each component. Lately, the airlines have employed this strategy to nail passengers with bag fees, seat upgrade fees, aisle seat upgrades, meal upgrades, and fees for just about everything short of oxygen.

Unbundling goes hand in hand with a psychological trick known as anchoring. The ploy here is to highly advertise the price for the most basic, stripped down level of service or product, while knowing full well that almost no one will ever get away with that price. The consumer, however, anchors on this advertised price and psychologically uses it to make competitive comparisons — even when they know that this price is a come-on. Yes, anchoring is that powerful.

Introductory pricing

You're probably familiar with Internet service offers from cable and phone companies, which offer a very attractive price for a limited time period followed by some contract requirement at the regular price for an additional, much longer period of time. It is nearly impossible to unravel the true cost once the introductory period ends as these companies bury that information in fine print and insist that "it varies with each customer" or run the consumer around between departments should they attempt to nail down the true cost.

Branding

Even branding can be categorized as a psychological tactic nowadays. Whereas a brand used to stand for high quality and consistency, now it mostly means higher prices. Generics in almost every consumable category from cereals to drugs to beauty products are proving to be much better values, and in many cases indistinguishable from the branded version. The value in most brands today lies in creating the impression in the consumer's mind that their product or service is hipper or sexier than their competitors. Apple is the poster child for this tactic.

Eco-friendly

Who says? Largely, this is just another tactic to capitalize on a fashionable trend. In some particularly egregious cases, the eco product or service is even less ecologically sound than the non-eco competitor. Waste companies use this tactic by offering recycling services, and then dumping the carefully sorted refuse in the same landfill with all the other garbage.

Deliberate misdirection

Any business, product, or service whose advertisements include the words 'value', 'bargain', 'affordable', 'economical' and so on, typically isn't. These businesses hope to discourage you from shopping any further, by their claim as the price leader. What you get is either not the lowest priced, or in some cases, a flawed copy.

Walmart is a good example. While they freely advertise "everyday low prices" they are not saying that everything they have is priced the lowest. In fact, with the exception of carefully selected items chosen to draw traffic, many of the other products are priced the same or higher than the competition.

Fighting back

As a consumer, your strongest weapon lies in recognizing these tactics for what they are — consumer psychological warfare. All of these tactics attempt to convince you to pay more for what in many cases amounts to a commodity. In other words, these businesses are trying to create some level of monopoly so they can increase prices and reduce customer service, and even product and service quality.

Because these tactics are ever evolving, you cannot simply learn a set of defensive strategies. You need to recognize that you are being manipulated. You should see any of these marketing ploys as red flags. In a way, these businesses, by the very fact that they resort to these tactics, are telling you that they have a commodity product or service. That is your cue to go for the lowest price. And, while you might lend some small weight to their claims of service or reputation, truly innovative product or service features are rarely a factor. Price, price, price must be your mantra.

Beyond resisting these psychological strikes, you must be willing to risk shopping the generic competition. Do not assume that a lower market profile — less promotion and advertising — equates to an inferior product or service. Start with some small purchases and convince yourself. Try a generic grocery product next time you're in the store. You'll be surprised at the quality of these substitutes. Once you see this for yourself, you can move on to generic tires, pest control, drugs, beauty products, oil changes, hand tools, outdoor grills, and thousands of other products and services. Yes, sometimes you will get burned, but for the overwhelming majority of the time you will save big, and never miss the more expensive, branded alternative.

Don't be buffaloed into paying more than you must. It's a game and you can play it, too. And here's the irony in it; most generics are manufactured by the same companies that promote the exclusiveness of their brands. Need some convincing? Sears Kenmore appliances, as an example, are made by Whirlpool and Maytag. Sears doesn't manufacture a blessed thing. Walmart's Great Value bacon — Tyson's, Great Value vegetables — Libby's, Great Value ice cream — Blue Bunny. And the list goes on and on. Sometimes the branded product is made to different specifications; however, in a lot of cases, there is no difference, except in price.

How about those times when you find yourself up against situational monopolies, such as the local auto repair shop or the contractor that can't seem to provide the true cost of their service or product upfront, claiming that "it all depends." You may have lots of choices before you commit, but once you do commit, watch out.

There are several ways to fight against these tactics. First and foremost is to do your homework. The more questions you ask, the less room you leave them to hit you with the usual line — "I didn't know about this when I quoted you the price." In essence you have to nail down the various components of the service to keep their wiggle room to a minimum. If they give you a one price quote, get them to break it down into pieces. Such things as fuel surcharges, trip charges, estimation fees, permit acquisition, diagnostic fees, and so on shouldn't be job dependent. Get these charges established upfront.

Unfortunately, the only way to win this game is to shop several competitors and compare the product or service pieces until you understand what components and prices you can identify. If you can't get a straight answer, take that as a red flag and move on. Check with various online reference sites such as Yelp, Google, and Angie's List. Pay particular attention to claims of "surprise charges." Also, be suspicious of website customer references maintained by the business itself, the temptation to pick and choose customer feedback for their in-house websites is often just too tempting.

Unfortunately, you can't avoid all consumer manipulation. After all, businesses do this sort of thing all the time; you are just a one-off amateur. You should build in an expectation that you will sometimes lose, and in some cases, it may not even be worth the effort to win. Generally, for purchases below $50, it probably isn't worth it. Up to $100, you will want to dig deeper. Over $100 and you should consider it all-out warfare — may the best man or woman win. Don't rush to buy or commit until you feel that the business is trustworthy and their product or service represents the best value.

Summary

The brave new world of consumer manipulation is upon us. Businesses understand psychological ploys and willingly employ them. As a consumer, you have the absolute right to pick and choose with whom to do business. Don't surrender this powerful weapon. There are almost no businesses without competition. Let your dollars do the walking and make sure that you get full value, before you sign on the dotted line.

2 Avoiding Money Disasters

Want to know the number one rule for building your wealth?

Don't lose what you have.

Sound obvious? Tell that to the 1.3 million people who, according to the American Bankruptcy Institute, will file for bankruptcy in 2013. Or, the 670,000 home owners who went through home foreclosure in 2012. This prescription is so simple, and so often overlooked that it should be plastered on refrigerators and home office walls across America. Moreover, the less you have, the more you should pay attention to this humble bit of wisdom.

Of course, not every bankruptcy and foreclosure could have been prevented with better financial management. But, how many bankruptcies could have been prevented by anticipating potential financial reverses, instead of expecting the best-case scenario to continue indefinitely? How many people are living on the brink of financial disaster, and don't even know it? How many home foreclosures might have been prevented had their owners realized that homes also lose value?

Want to avoid a financial meltdown? Start with the realization that it can happen to you, no matter how financially secure you may be. In fact, being financially secure may actually increase your risk of incurring some of the potential catastrophes covered below.

Incidentally, not all financial reverses happen quickly. Some may not be immediately catastrophic, but in conjunction with other setbacks, can wind up destroying your financial well-being just the same.

Emergency cash reserve

This is the ultimate no brainer. Failing to have an adequate cash reserve is like playing Russian roulette with your wealth. Most everyone will experience a financial reverse at some time, whether from illness, job loss, or unexpected expenses. In which case, you will need some ready cash to keep paying your bills until you can sort things out.

Most financial planners agree on a cash reserve equal to at least six months' worth of expenses. But don't let this put you off; any amount is better than nothing. This is your shock absorber in a very rough world.

Health insurance

There is disagreement over exactly how many bankruptcies arise as a direct result of uncovered medical expenses. During the debate over the Patient Protection and Affordable Care Act, also know as Obamacare, the claim was made that around 50% were attributable to healthcare costs. This number has since been disputed with subsequent studies suggesting that the number may be closer to 25%. Regardless of the exact figure, healthcare remains a potent wealth destroyer as well as a significant contributor, if not the major cause of bankruptcy.

Just to put things in perspective, the table below shows some of the most common emergency room visits and their associated charges based upon a National Institutes of Health study released in February 2013 encompassing over 8,000 emergency room visits by non-elderly (18-64 year-old) patents with a single discharge diagnosis. While these charges do not reflect the average, they do reflect actual charges that befell patients that were unlucky enough to choose the wrong (most expensive) hospital for treatment.

Table 2-1
Emergency Room Charges

Sprains and Strains	$24,111
Other Injury	$27,238
Open Wounds of Extremities	$25,863
Normal Pregnancy and or Delivery	$18,320
Headache	$17,797
Back Problems	$10,403
Upper Respiratory Infection	$17,421
Kidney Stone	$39,408
Urinary Tract Infection	$73,002
Intestinal Infection	$29,551

Worse still, a high number of those filing for bankruptcy attributable to medical costs, as high as 73% in one study, indicated that they had some form of medical insurance. This would certainly suggests that having healthcare insurance by itself is not enough. You must also plan for the high out-of-pocket expenses often built into such plans. After all, limiting maximum out-of-pocket expenses to $10,000 is $10,000 most people still don't have.

Healthcare insurance is much too specialized and information too quickly outdated to be addressed in any meaningful way in a general personal finance book. As of the date of this publication, new healthcare exchanges are slated to commence operations on October 1, 2013. For many, these state and federal exchanges will provide much needed access to healthcare insurance. Whether it will be affordable remains to be seen. Suffice it to say, going without it is taking a huge risk with your money, potentially wiping out everything you've accumulated from a lifetime of work.

Umbrella insurance

If you've been diligent about managing your money and built up some amount of savings, investments, or home equity, collectively called your assets, then your risk shifts toward protecting yourself from those who might want to take it from you. An umbrella liability policy essentially adds additional liability protection on top of your underlying policies for auto and homeowner's insurance. At a minimum, you should buy at least a $1,000,000 umbrella policy as it covers not only potential liability, but also the legal cost to defend yourself. Beyond this, you should buy liability insurance equal to or greater than your net worth. If you don't know how to calculate your net worth, don't worry as we'll cover that in Chapter 6. The annual cost of such coverage is generally modest, amounting to around $350 per million dollars of coverage as of the date of this publication.

Under insurance

Don't underestimate the cost of catastrophic losses to your home or business. If may be tempting to forgo flood insurance or not to keep your policy up to speed with rising replacement costs, but losses from a fire, flood, mudslide, or what have you will dwarf the costs of maintaining adequate insurance.

Pay the right bills on time

If you want to play this game, at least learn to play it properly. It is always best to pay all of your bills on time and in the full amount. However, sometimes life doesn't work out that way. You will want to read the chapters on credit scores and credit cards to help you prioritize your bills. You must always take into account such things as how often and how long ago you have failed to make timely payments. Don't treat all bills alike.

Generally speaking, you should select those bills with the least likelihood that the creditor will report you to a credit agency and will be the least disruptive to your lifestyle. Typically, entertainment expenses such as cable TV, Internet service, health club dues, etc. are the least disruptive; however, these providers can be swift to end your service for nonpayment. Payments to small businesses and landlords likewise can often be delayed if you communicate your financial problem to them and then carry through on any subsequent payment commitments. Alternately, making late payments on loans, mortgages, credit cards, and utilities is always a bad idea.

Identity theft

Although modern technology has provided great benefit, it has also imposed a huge cost by way of stolen identities and financial fraud. According to a report released by the Bureau of Justice Statistics, in 2010 an estimated 8.6 million households had at least one person age 12 or older who was a victim of identity theft resulting in an average household loss of

$2,200. Moreover, when stolen identity information was used to open a new account, the average loss ballooned to $13,000.

There are several simple things you can do to prevent financial identity theft. These will cost you little or nothing, except for a few minutes of your time.

1. Set up alerts at your bank to notify you of any suspicious activity in your accounts. For instance, you can set alerts when any of the following occur: a withdrawal of cash from an ATM, a charge is entered for more than an amount that you stipulate, like $100, and a change in the phone number or other information on your account.

2. Review your credit and bank accounts on line at least twice per month and scan for suspicious charges.

3. Buy a paper shredder and shred anything with credit sensitive information on it, such as your Social Security number, date of birth, bank account and credit card numbers.

4. Don't give out your Social Security number if you can possibly avoid it. Most businesses understand that consumers are reluctant to provide this information, so they will accommodate your wishes.

5. Install anti-virus/anti-spyware software on your computer and keep it updated.

6. Check your credit reports annually. You can check one of the three major credit reporting agencies —Experian,

TransUnion, and Equifax — each year for free at www. annualcreditreport.com.

7. Avoid using your debit card except for cash withdrawals at an ATM. See Chapter 4 for more on this. Instead, use your credit card instead, for as many purchases as possible.

8. Never give anyone your debit card PIN or access to your online accounts.

9. If you have lost your wallet or credit/debit cards, report them immediately. The limit of your losses depends upon how quickly you report them lost or stolen.

10. If you suspect that you may be the victim of identity theft, place a freeze on your credit information. This will prevent someone from opening a new account in your name, which as shown previously can result in the greatest consumer losses.

Overconfidence effect

The overconfidence effect is a well established psychological bias wherein people's confidence in their subjective judgment far exceeds the actual outcomes. For example, in one study, participants were asked to estimate a certain quantity, say the total egg production in the U.S., or the total number of physicians and surgeons in the Boston Yellow Pages. Even though the participants felt that their answers were accurate within 2%, in actuality their error rate was 46%. (This and other common biases are covered in detail in Chapter 10 Investor Psychology.)

Psychologists have called the overconfidence effect the most 'pervasive and potentially catastrophic' of all the cognitive biases to which human beings fall victim. It has been blamed for lawsuits, strikes, wars, and stock market bubbles and crashes.

Overconfidence, in combination with managing your money, can be equally disastrous. Believing with a high degree of certainty that good things will happen more often, and bad things less, will lead you to ignore the potential for financial disaster, including the list of catastrophes mentioned in this chapter. Over-optimism can lead to either the denial of your financial situation or to the belief that you'll always find a way to make expensive house payments or car payments; no matter what financial setbacks befall you.

The best course is to expect that things will not always go your way. How much these setbacks will cost you is anyone's guess; however, if you at least cover the potential for a financial catastrophe, you can greatly reduce your risk of being wiped out.

Watch out for toxic friends

Your friends may be your worst enemy, when it comes to your finances. This doesn't mean that you should abandon your friends, only that you should think twice before you buy a new car, or a bigger house, or an expensive vacation based upon impressing them. At the end of the day, your friends will not be impressed, usually because they are too busy trying to impress you. More than likely you will only succeed in escalating the race to live beyond your means.

Slow down

This may sound like odd, even quaint advice in this day of instant 24/7 communication, but the rules of money management have changed little in the last twenty or even one-hundred years.

When it comes to your money, avoid making snap decisions.

You'll find most deadlines, except for those related to paying your bills, are manufactured to rush you into making a decision without considering the true consequences or searching for better alternatives. Come-ons such as 'limited quantities', 'act now', 'offer expires soon', 'low introductory price', 'today only', and on and on are meant to overpower your rational mind with your emotions. It's amazing and laughable how many of these one-time opportunities come around again and again, usually the very next week.

If you fall for these, at best you will waste a little money; at worst, you will find yourself losing your hard-earned savings. Remember, you have the cash; you are in control. It's the business trying to sell you something that doesn't have the cash. In this economy, cash wins. Don't give away your advantage.

Read the fine print

Know what you're getting into whenever you commit to a long-term contract. Don't just look at the monthly payments, assuming that as long as they fit your budget, you'll be okay.

If you read nothing else, at least understand the penalties

should you terminate your contract early or fail to make a payment. Credit card agreements, cell phone contracts, auto loans, mortgages, and rental agreements can, and do contain severe financial penalties should you fail to perform as agreed.

All those little things

As promised, here is a list of some useful little things that you can easily forget about or ignore, but that can have an outsize impact on your finances.

- Hang up on cold calls to your home
- Don't risk your health, it's never worth it
- Pay your bills on time
- Don't drive on worn-out tires.
- Change your oil in your car at least every six months.
- Keep all your important papers collected together in one place.
- Don't forget to renew your driver's license.
- Never drive your car without liability insurance.
- If you own a business with employees, never fail to pay your payroll taxes.
- Always pay your income taxes on time.
- Don't believe anyone who promises to double your tax refund.
- Replace worn washing machine hoses.
- Never write a bad check.

- Don't drive drunk.

- Never miss a payment for your insurance.

- Don't speed.

- Call your mother.

Summary

Life is full of risks. However, in our modern world, you can thrive in spite of them. Don't let your belief that "it won't happen to me" rob you of your financial future. Remember the number one rule for building wealth; don't lose what you have.

3   Keeping It Simple

In this chapter, we'll examine a case study in practical, personal finance in action. We'll be following the story of Jason and Tiffany, an American, middle-class couple, both in their late thirties. You may have more resources or fewer than this couple, or you may be older or younger; but as you'll see, the same principles still apply.

A practical example

Jason and Tiffany will demonstrate the powerful financial benefits resulting from the thoughtful application of only a handful of the many financial concepts covered in this book. Pay particular attention to the process they employ to develop their financial plan, as this will serve as a template you can use to achieve your own financial goals.

Jason works as a supervisor for a small manufacturer, making $48,000 per year salary. His wife, Tiffany, is a stay-at-home mom with a ten-year-old daughter. Tiffany makes some crafts and sells them on her Etsy Internet store. Her annual income is less than $1,000. Jason has been laid off periodically over the years, so he and Tiffany haven't been able to accumulate a lot of money for retirement or emergencies. They don't live extravagantly, but they do manage to take an annual vacation, provided Jason is employed. If not, then they take a stay-cation and make the best of things.

Jason and Tiffany bought a new home about five years ago with a small down payment, and owing to the recent recession, they are underwater on their mortgage. Home prices have risen somewhat in the last year, but not enough to reach break-even with what they paid. Selling their house in order to move would be a real hardship for them.

Neither Jason nor Tiffany are living the life of their dreams. They feel stuck and the future looks a lot like the past. They have a vague plan to move somewhere else after their daughter graduates from high school. Paying for her college isn't even on their radar screen.

Jason and Tiffany are very much like today's typical American family. Their lives are okay as long as the main breadwinner remains employed, but they have this gnawing sense of insecurity about their future. They recognize that improving their finances would help alleviate their fears, but they don't know where to begin.

Now this is where most finance books would launch into a financial checklist suggesting that this couple reduce credit card debt, eliminate wasteful spending, and increase their savings. All worthwhile ideas, to be sure, but somewhat akin to writing a prescription for a patient who is still sitting in the waiting room.

In essence, Jason and Tiffany really have only three money management/lifestyle choices. One is to keep on keeping on. The second is to rearrange their spending. The third is to find a way to increase their income. They can work these choices in any combination, but that's really the range of their options. It's not rocket science.

What they choose to do will then determine their money

management plan. If they choose to stick with the status quo, then they need do nothing. They are intentionally choosing to live with insecurity and unfulfilled potential. So be it.

The other alternatives require some decisions as to what they want from life. While we may be victims of our circumstances in the short term, all of us have a choice in the long term. For example, Jason and Tiffany may decide that their income is adequate to meet their life's goals if only they could figure out how to better manage what they have. Or they may decide that they will never get what they want out of life without more drastic changes, such as a relocation, a better-paying job, or maybe a job for Tiffany. In this instance, they have to decide how much they are willing to disrupt their lives to achieve their goals.

These are choices we all face. If life isn't what we had hoped for, and we aren't willing to do anything about it, then we need do nothing. That's easy, isn't it? Otherwise, we are forced to decide what makes our lives more fulfilling, and then make a plan to get there.

You can see that money management prescriptions are nearly useless unless you can first define how you want to live. If you can't stand to shop garage sales and pinch pennies, then you will need to look to other ways to support your lifestyle goals. If such things bother you not in the least, then extreme savings strategies may well allow you to accomplish your financial plan. The basic principle is this:

> *Any money management plan that doesn't fit how you want to live your life is a setup to fail.*

A lot of people believe that if they just have more knowledge, more specialized money management tools at their disposal, then their lives and finances can be improved. This may be so for a short-term fix, but in the long term, it will not be sustainable. Making lifestyle choices that you can commit to (and live with) is far more important.

Returning to Jason and Tiffany, suppose that they decide that of all the things they might do to improve their lives, eliminating the anxiety over Jason's recurring layoffs would top the list. Translating their desire into a financial goal is the very first step in the process. Without spending a great deal of time crunching numbers, they calculate that $10,000 in savings, or about six months' worth of expenses, would be adequate to insulate them against the worst of the financial hardships of unemployment. It's better to set a good-enough goal, rather than waste a lot of time micro-tuning one that can be adjusted endlessly in the future.

Now let's look at how they might develop a sustainable money management plan to support this simple savings goal.

- Keep it simple. The more moving pieces, the more difficult it will be to track and adjust.

- Identify some lifestyle changes that will yield real financial results and place a dollars and cents number on each.

- Total the amount each option adds toward achieving the goal.

- Pick those lifestyle changes that have the least impact while maintaining real progress toward the financial goal.

- Be prepared to revisit the plan as often as necessary should some new options present themselves or other choices prove to be too difficult to sustain.

This is the process that Jason and Tiffany used. Here are some of their lifestyle options that they considered. Initially, they each considered working more to increase their income. And although extra income would solve a lot of problems, neither of them wanted to make the requisite lifestyle changes. Jason liked his free time, while Tiffany had no interest in returning to work.

Likewise, they considered and rejected Jason's finding another, better-paying job. That would require relocation without any guarantee of success, along with selling their house at a loss. Neither of which would guarantee that these sacrifices would payoff.

That left only the option to alter their spending. The first place they looked was for those lifestyle choices, which by themselves were not expensive or wasteful, but which leverage more wasteful spending. For example, everyone knows a new car comes with a hefty price tag, but what they fail to consider is the cost of sales taxes, license fees, and auto insurance that comes along with new car ownership.

You can look for these packages of expenses in your own spending. It could be as simple as patronizing a Starbucks co-located with a Barnes & Noble. You may go into Starbucks for a latte and come out with a magazine and a book. As you learned from Chapter One, that's the way it's designed to work. Not to pick on Starbucks and Barnes & Noble, but it demonstrates how one lifestyle choice inadvertently leads to another and another. Eliminate one and you can multiply the financial benefit.

Jason and Tiffany place Tiffany's three-year-old Lexus with a hefty auto loan into that category. One possibility, is to trade in the Lexus and get a used Hyundai Santa Fe, thereby freeing up a total about $300 per month in car payments. This may be an unacceptable alternative for some, but then they have to ask themselves if this is a lifestyle impact or an ego impact?

They also find that Jason likes to eat lunch out every day. Adding up the expenses, they see that he could save about $100 per month by brown-bagging it. Once again, would eliminating some of these lunch expenses create a significant lifestyle impact?

CLEM expenses

Typically, wasteful packages or bundles of expenses are the result of one of the following, which can collectively be termed CLEM spending. It would be a good bet that everyone, no matter how frugal, has some CLEM expenses hiding in their spending.

C	Convenience — spending driven by location and familiarity
L	Laziness — as in not doing your homework to find the cheapest deal
E	Ego – spending driven by bragging rights and prestige
M	Momentum – spending with businesses that unreasonably raise prices or force their customers into more expensive 'value' packages

Here are some of the CLEM expenses that Jason and Tiffany found as they dug through their spending habits.

- A $26 six-month oil change that has morphed into a $45 every-three-month-under-your-hood jackpot. (Convenience, Momentum)

- Jason's barber who has increased his prices from $30.00 to $50.00 in the last two years. (Momentum)

- The upscale, $12.00, blue-moon, eco-friendly margarita that has replaced the $6.00 house margarita at their favorite bar. (Momentum, Ego)

- The summer lawn service at $50.00 per mow is now a year-round $1,000 package complete with aeration, spraying, fertilizing, and snow plowing. (Convenience, Momentum)

- The pest company that used to come out and spray once in the spring for $50, but now charges $250 for four applications per year. (Convenience, Momentum)

- The free, three-month HBO package is now a $20.00 per month necessity. (Momentum)

- The fill-up at the local gas station now includes a bi-monthly $5.00 car wash. (Convenience, Ego)

- Replacing their running shoes every six months migrated from that neon green $50 pair to the $95 model. (Ego)

- The monthly cell phone overages and roaming charges went from $0 to $20.00. (Laziness)

- The membership in the health club that no one uses now costs $50 a month along with regular annual increases. (Momentum)

- Shopping at Walmart was just too humiliating and the other grocery stores offer a better selection. (Ego, Momentum)

You may disagree with this couple's list of CLEM expenses, but most everyone would agree that they have a few of their own. If you want to manage your money for the long term, you must guard against these money vampires, because they can add up quickly. What's amazing is that reducing these expenses, or even eliminating them, often results in very little impact on your lifestyle. Let's face it. Beyond spending for food, shelter, transportation, and a job, most every expense is some form of CLEM spending.

Beyond the necessities of life, most spending is driven by some combination of Convenience, Laziness, Ego, or Momentum or CLEM.

After considering their CLEM expenses, Jason and Tiffany realize that having the ultimate financial benefits far outweigh the hassles of reducing or eliminating them.

Based upon this list of options, they can now make a dollar and cents plan. They don't need to clip coupons, move into a cheap apartment, wear secondhand clothes, or make any other drastic adjustment. They also have no need to keep elaborate spreadsheets, nor dig through a year's worth of receipts to make an extensive budget. All they need to do is follow the simple plan shown below. Nothing more is required.

After jockeying the numbers a little bit, here is how Jason and Tiffany decided to save $10,000 in two years.

Table 3-1

Simple Financial Plan to Save $10,000 in 24 Months

	Monthly Savings	Total After 24 months
Financial Goal	$417	$10,000
Trade in Lexus	300	7,200
Cancel Health Club	50	1,200
Eliminate HBO	20	480
New Cell Phone Plan	20	480
Shop for Pest Service	15	600
Misc. Savings	17	408
Total	$417	$10,008

Here is the beauty of this approach.

1. It's simple. Jason and Tiffany have a clearly defined goal with a simple plan to get there. Most of these changes require nothing more than shopping around a little in the beginning along with an ongoing commitment to stick with the changes.

2. It's supported by their lifestyle. They don't have to work extra hours, or at all in Tiffany's case. They don't have to spend their weekends shopping for hot bargains. They don't have to make big sacrifices. In other words, their plan is free of all those things that make most plans so onerous and doomed to fail.

3. It's manageable. The goal is big enough to be meaningful and yet small enough to be realized in a reasonable amount of time along with a reasonable amount of effort.

4. In twenty-four months, it's over. They can see progress against their goal, and they know it will eventually end. Once it's over, they can return to their old ways with an extra $10,000 in the bank.

5. Yes, they still have to cut expenses; this is the real world. But it's all about cutting the right expenses that makes this plan work.

A sustainable money management plan is the result of small, well-considered steps, not sweeping changes. Unless your finances are in shambles, such crash programs just don't work. People's lifestyles evolved over time, so the same slow evolution is the best way to change them when establishing a financial plan.

Also, the fewer lifestyle changes you need to make to achieve your goals, the better. It's easier to track. It's easier to implement; it's easier to sustain. Lasting change takes effort, so the fewer such changes the better.

As you can see, this is a pretty simple plan. Jason and Tiffany can write this one out on a piece of paper and stick it on their refrigerator. It's surprising how motivational it can be to see progress against your goals. As one goal is achieved, the next can be substituted in its place. Jason and Tiffany may decide to keep going after they have saved the cash for their emergency fund, using the same plan to buy new furniture. Don't underestimate the impact of little changes over time. Here's how this could play out if they continued on this plan for three more years. They would have accumulated a cash cushion of $10,000, plus $2,000 for new furniture, and another $3,000 to help pay for their daughter's college education.

Your lifestyle choices will be different from Jason's and Tiffany's. And your financial plan will be different as well. You maybe an extreme shopper who can find hundreds of dollars of savings through shrewd shopping or maybe you don't mind making more extreme lifestyle changes, such as giving up your car. That's great. You may choose to save for a down payment for a house, or a new car, or a big vacation, or to pay off your credit cards. If you've read any other finance books you know the rewards stemming from paying off credit cards, a topic explored in more depth in Appendix A — Compound Interest

Once you have identified a life-fulfilling goal and placed a financial value on it, there remains any number of ways to achieve it, any of which can be altered over time as circumstances change. You may find that some lifestyle changes aren't sustainable; this is normal. Perhaps giving up HBO is just too hard. Then review your spending and try something else. Or maybe you can find an additional source of savings. The main thing is to keep sight of your goal and keep moving toward it.

Summary

In this chapter you have seen how one couple has chosen to apply a small fraction of the many financial tools covered in this book. As you look to apply these in your own life, keep the following points in mind.

1. Identify a goal that will improve your life and then place a dollar amount on that goal. What you chose is entirely

up to you. It's your life. If you want to save up to buy
a collection of comic books, instead of paying off your
credit cards, then that's what you should do.

2.   Identify any number of options that will help you reach
     that goal in a reasonable amount of time.

3.   Pick the options that have the highest payback with the
     least amount of lifestyle sacrifice. Don't turn your life
     into a treadmill to feed your finances.

4.   When you reach your goal, feel free to stop. The end is
     one of the rewards.

5.   This is a long-term process designed to yield worthwhile
     results. Like turning a barge in the river, your present
     financial situation will improve if you have a plan and
     stick to it. Don't sabotage your future success by trying
     to make drastic changes. You will quickly grow to resent
     the effort, and lose interest.

In the end, practical money management means making
smart moves, not radical, short-term fixes. As you will see
in the following chapters, successful personal finance comes
down to knowing what moves to make and when. Save the
sweat and effort for your workouts.

4   Read This Before You Swipe That Card

If you're like most people, there's a good chance you have
a credit card or two, a debit card, a checkbook stuffed into
a desk drawer, and maybe even a PayPal account for making
online purchases. You probably also have some form of
automatic withdrawal tied to your checking account to
pay your monthly bills. You may think that all of these
payment options are only different flavors of the same thing.
You simply choose one or the other depending upon the
circumstance or your convenience.

However, each of these means to move your money around
works in a different way and more importantly, affords you
very different protections should you be unhappy with your
purchase or should your credit information falls into the
wrong hands.

Here's an example. Let's suppose you pull up to a gas pump
and decide to use your debit card, instead of your credit card.
Since it's a few days before payday, you have just enough in
your account to buy $25.00 of gas – enough to get by until you
actually get your paycheck.

Later, when you go to the bank to deposit your paycheck,
you're shocked to find that the charge for the gas you thought
was $25.00 is $75.00 instead. And to make matters worse,
you have also incurred a $35.00 overdraft fee. Welcome to the
world of electronic banking.

Before we get into the details as to why this can happen,
let's begin with some basics. Even readers with a lifetime

of experience in managing their bank accounts will find the following information to be a real eye-opener.

Checking accounts

The good old-fashioned checking account is the foundation of all modern electronic forms of funds transfer (moving your money electronically). A checking account is essentially an agreement between you and your bank, which allows the bank to use your money until you ask for it back. You can ask for it back whenever you want, called making demand for it, in any number of ways, including writing a check, swiping your debit card, clicking on a smartphone app, and so on.

Electronic Funds Transfer background

Up until 2004, all checks had to physically travel from the merchant to whom you wrote a check, to their bank, and then to your bank where the check was *cleared;* provided you had sufficient money in your checking account or *bounced* back to the merchant's bank stamped NSF meaning *not sufficient funds.* All of this took time and cost a lot of money to administer. In 2004, a new federal law *Check 21* allowed banks to substitute a digital image for the physical check, thereby allowing banks to move checks electronically. And that changed everything, as the saying goes.

Credit cards and debit cards

Let's begin with the two most familiar means of electronic fund transfer — credit cards and debit cards. Although you use both of these by swiping them through a card reader, at heart they are very different.

Debit cards withdraw money from your checking account,
while credit cards use money lent to you from the bank
or other card issuer.

As you know, credit cards require your signature to validate a purchase, while debit cards use a personal identification number or PIN. Since a debit card withdraws funds from your checking account almost instantaneously, you must have sufficient funds in your account before you use it. Should you choose to use it anyway, the transaction will either be denied or you will be charged an overdraft fee.

A credit card, on the other hand, results in a loan to you from your bank or card issuer, which in turn, you will need to repay with interest. Much is made about the evils of credit cards; however, credit cards are far from evil. They are just a tool. It's only when these modern-payment conveniences are misused that problems arise.

While it is true that credit cards carry a high interest rate and the penalties for missing payments can be severe, they also provide some very powerful benefits that don't come with cash, checks, or debit cards.

The grace period

One of the most useful features, found on most all credit cards, is the 21 to 25-day interest-free grace period commencing from each month's statement date. Any charges made during the previous month can be paid off within this grace period without interest. In other words, you get to use the bank's money without cost. Given the superior fraud protections (explained below) and interest-free grace period, you should use your credit card to the fullest extent possible — with one major caution. You must pay off all of your charges every month within the grace period, otherwise, like any powerful medicine, this one can be toxic to your finances.

With interest rates of 12%, 18%, and even 24%, carrying a balance for even a short period of time will be very costly. Make the minimum payment on a balance of $1,000 and it will take 9½ years to pay it off. Your total interest charges will nearly equal the amount you initially borrowed.

If you treat credit cards with the respect they deserve; however, in addition to the grace period, you can also enjoy cash-back rewards, airline bonus miles, and various merchant discounts, which makes using your credit card as much as possible the best choice. One again, this doesn't mean you should run up your credit card debt as much as possible, only that you should use your credit card as much as possible provided you pay off the balance every month. Don't confuse the two.

Consumer protections

Debit and credit cards also differ in how much they protect you, either from misuse of your card by others or misuse by those merchants with whom you do business. In fact, debit and credit cards are even covered by different laws.

Credit cards, having been around longer than debit cards, are covered by the 1975 Fair Credit Billing Act, while debit cards are covered by the Electronic Fund Transfer Act of 1978. You may be thinking *so what* at this point, but here's where all this means something to you.

In general, your losses from the unauthorized use of your credit cards are limited to $50.00, whereas your losses from debit cards can be unlimited.

Does that get your attention? Here's how it works.

Unauthorized use of your credit card

If someone steals, borrows, or otherwise uses your credit card without your permission, you are only liable for $50 of the charges, regardless of how much has been charged. You are not liable for any amount at all if you report the card stolen before any charges are incurred, because your credit card company will cancel the card before it can be used.

Billing errors

If a merchant overcharges your account for goods or services, or charges you for something you never received, then the provisions of the Fair Credit Billing Act force your credit card issuer to follow specific procedures to investigate and resolve the dispute. Often you can initiate this process with a phone call; however, for the full protection of the law you must submit a written letter to your credit card company within 60 days of the first incorrect billing statement. The letter must be sent certified mail, return receipt requested, and include the following:

- your name and account number,
- the dollar amount of the charge you dispute,

- a statement of the reason you dispute the charge (unauthorized charge, did not receive purchased item, did not receive credit after a return, charged more than agreed amount, etc).

Your credit card company must provide an address on its billing statement to which you can send dispute letters.

Stop payment on your credit card

One of the best benefits of using credit cards is your ability to stop payment when you are dissatisfied with something you have purchased. You can employ this feature if there is a legitimate problem with the quality of goods or services you purchased, as long as you've made an effort to resolve the issue with the merchant first. When you notify your credit card company that you are withholding payment for the particular charge, they in turn cannot report that amount as delinquent to a credit bureau until the dispute is settled, or a court judgment is issued against you.

Technically, the purchase must be for more than $50.00 and within 100 miles of your home, but few credit card companies enforce this provision. However, you should know that it is their choice and a credit card issuer can choose to enforce these restrictions if they desire.

Stopping payment is particularly beneficial for online purchases. Online merchants who accept credit cards are generally treated as guilty until proven innocent, at least when it comes to credit card disputes. Without an actual signature on a sales receipt, they have no acceptable evidence to present should a customer claim that they didn't actually place an order. Even if a customer signs a receipt for goods they received from an online merchant, the customer can still claim that they mistakenly signed for the receipt without knowing the contents of the shipment, and the credit card company will accept this defense. Even worse for the merchant, the customer is under no obligation to return that same merchandise. As you can well guess, this sort of consumer power can be easily abused.

Debit cards

The law pertaining to the use of debit cards, the Electronic Funds Transfer Act of 1978, differs from credit cards, and in general, provides fewer consumer protections. Because of this, coupled with the fact that debit cards are a direct pipeline into your checking account, use of your debit card should be restricted exclusively to cash withdrawals at the ATM.

Unauthorized use of your debit card

If you notify your bank before your lost or stolen debit card is used, you won't incur any losses. In order to limit your losses to $50.00 as with credit cards, you must notify your bank within two business days of discovering an unauthorized transaction, whether from a lost or stolen card or other billing mistakes. If you wait up to sixty days, you loss could be a much as $500. Beyond sixty days, your losses may be unlimited, including everything in your checking account along with your overdraft protection, or even a savings account tied to your checking account.

Stop payment on your debit card

Sorry, unless you are very fast, as in seconds of the transaction, you cannot cancel a debit card transaction. That's because once the charge hits your bank account, the funds are removed instantly. Your only recourse is to work something out with the merchant. You do not have the option to stop payment as with a credit card. For this reason alone, you should never use a debit card to make an online purchase.

Never use your debit card for online purchases.

Debit card hold

If you decide to use your debit card to purchase gasoline, for example, you may be surprised when the merchant places a preauthorization hold, or a temporary restriction, on your checking account for a sum of money greater than the purchase. When a merchant cannot know beforehand how much you might charge, as when you use a debit card to purchase gas, they are allowed to estimate the amount in order to cover themselves when the real charge is known. While the merchant estimates the amount, your bank determines the amount of time this restriction stays in place on your account, which can be for several days. The result is that the $25.00 of gas you purchased may result in a $75.00 hold. If the balance in your checking account is low, you may inadvertently trigger an overdraft fee.

ATM cards

When ATM cards first arrived on the scene, they were intended for withdrawing cash from your checking account at ATM machines. Over time these cards morphed into debit cards as banks added more features, until they could move money around the same as if they were credit cards. But as you have seen, a debit card is not a credit card.

The good old ATM card, as opposed to the debit card, still exists and is a better choice to keep you out of trouble. Since you should restrict the use of your debit card to ATM withdrawals anyway, it might make more sense to request an ATM card in the first place.

Recent changes in credit card laws

Fed up with some of the tricks that banks had used to drive up customer fees for overdrafts and late payments, Congress enacted the Credit Card Accountability, Responsibility and Disclosure Act or CARD Act in 2009. Under the provisions of this new law, credit card users gained some new protections — not from the potential misuse of their cards, but from the banks and card issuers themselves.

- Late payment fees are limited to $25.00 unless one of your last six payments was late, in which case the fee may be up to $35.
- Your credit card issuer cannot charge you an inactivity fee — meaning a charge if you do not use your card.
- Your credit card issuer cannot charge a late fee greater than the minimum payment. For example, they cannot charge you a $25.00 late fee for a $10 minimum payment.
- Prior to the CARD act, along with a late fee, card issuers would also increase the interest rate on all previous

charges carried as your credit card balance. Under the new law, the increased interest rate applies only to new charges and must be reevaluated every six months to determine if the rate is still justified.

- Credit card issuers cannot allow you to exceed your credit card limit (and charge you a penalty fee) unless you specifically agree in writing.

Some of the popular newer products

Every year, banks and others outside of the finance industry invent more ways to help you move your money around. While they all use electronic funds transfer, these new services shouldn't be mistaken for bank-issued credit cards and debit cards. Here's what you need to know about a few of the more popular new products.

Prepaid debit cards

Often featured at convenience stores and big retailers like Walmart, non-bank issued, prepaid debit cards offer many conveniences for customers lacking a checking account. You buy prepaid credit cards at their face value, such as $25, $100 or more, and then use them like a regular debit card until the face value amount has been spent. Some allow you to refill them by paying more money, which you can then again spend down to a balance of zero.

Very often, these cards come with lots of fees. They almost always require an activation fee, which can be as high as $10, along with balance inquiry fees, monthly maintenance fees, inactivity fees, and even customer service fees. All these fees can make them an extremely expensive way to spend your cash electronically.

Lately, banks have started issuing prepaid debit cards as well. J.P. Morgan Chase now offers a prepaid debit card with no charge for activation, transactions, bill payment, or customer service. Additionally, the card can be used at any of the Chase branch ATMs. Other banks, such as PNC and Regions, also offer cards; however, these banks do not have as many ATM and branch locations.

For those without a banking relationship, these low-fee, prepaid debit cards may be a worthwhile alternative. Keep in mind, they will not help you to build a credit history, which in today's world can negatively impact your access to future credit, your ability to buy a house, or even lengthen the odds of landing a job.

Echecks/ACH

If you've ever written a check to Walmart, you might have been curious as to why they didn't keep your check. Instead, they scan it and hand it back to you. In the process, they also void your check, so that it can't be used again. This electronic conversion of your paper check to an echeck allows them to avoid the hassle of handling your physical check. However, they still use the same clearing process as for paper checks, known as ACH or Automated Clearing House, resulting in the same processing time as a physical check. Unlike your debit card, an echeck charge is not instantaneously applied to your checking account. In addition, you won't get a copy of your check back in your bank statement (although, you will see the amount charged), so be sure to keep a copy of your cancelled check for your records.

Automatic withdrawal

You may be one of the many who have chosen to tie an automatic withdrawal program to your banking accounts. As you know, automatic withdrawal electronically transfers money from your checking account to another account on a recurring basis, requiring no action on your part. Utilities, phone companies, cable and satellite TV, just to mention a few, all encourage you to use automatic withdrawal. "Just sign up once and forget about the hassle of paying monthly bills," they claim. To initiate the process, you signed an agreement authorizing these merchants to make a direct withdrawal from your checking or credit card account to pay their monthly bill. It can be a convenience, but it also carries a degree of risk. Among these is the risk that an automatic withdrawal will hit your checking account at the wrong time, resulting in an overdraft.

The greater risk; however, lies in trying to stop automatic withdrawals, should you have a problem. If you have an automatic withdrawal agreement, and for whatever reason; there is an error or a disputed charge, you cannot ask the bank to stop future withdrawals. Automatic withdrawal agreements are between you and the merchant, not between you and the bank. The bank cannot interfere with the agreement as they were not a part of it. The bank is only acting on your instructions as authorized in the automatic withdrawal agreement. In order to stop automatic withdrawals, you must get the merchant to agree to stop billing you. If they are unscrupulous, which is possible with some Internet businesses, you may have a difficult time doing this. Worse yet, even if you close your account, automatic withdrawals can still be held against you.

If you can't end the agreement, you can stop payment on automatic withdrawal payments; however, the stop-payment order is only good for one transaction at a time. Here is how the process works, according to the U.S. Treasury (www. treasury.gov).

"To stop payment, you will need to notify the bank at least three business days before the transaction is scheduled to be made (the automatic withdrawal). Notice may be made orally or in writing. However, if the notice is made orally, the bank may require you to follow up with written notice within 14 days. If you don't provide written verification of the oral notice when required, the oral stop payment order ceases to be effective."

On top of all this, your bank may charge you a fee for each stop-payment order. You should be very careful with automatic withdrawal agreements, limiting their use to only those businesses and individuals you trust. If possible, don't enter into these agreements at all.

A much better way: online bill payment

Instead of automatic withdrawal, you should use your bank's electronic bill payment system, which is termed a *push* process, as opposed to automatic withdrawal, which is termed a *pull* process. As we just discussed, automatic withdrawal allows a merchant to pull money from your account whenever they elect. In a push process, you must first authorize any withdrawals. In essence, you push the money out of your account.

Banks have different names for this service, but it is most commonly referred to as online bill payment. To initiate the service, your bank will require you to provide the payment details for the merchants and service providers you wish to include. The bank will only release funds after you have approved the payment of their invoices. Some banks require you to manually enter the billing amount and authorize every payment. Others have more automated systems. Whichever online bill service you use, consider any inconvenience as a small price to pay to protect your bank account from unauthorized use.

PayPal

If you've ever purchased anything from eBay, you are familiar with PayPal. It is yet another electronic fund transfer service, except that PayPal is not associated with any bank. Instead, PayPal acts as a middleman between your bank and the seller. This service offers a higher level of protection for your financial information, because the merchant never has access to your checking or credit card information. Unlike making a purchase at a store, where you hand over your credit card to the merchant or swipe it through their terminal, this never happens with PayPal. Instead, you give your financial information to PayPal. They, in turn, conduct the transaction with the seller on your behalf. As a consumer, PayPal costs you nothing extra as the seller pays all of the PayPal service fee.

To set up a PayPal account, you first give PayPal access to either your credit card or your bank account, to which they will pass along charges from the merchant. While there is a definite benefit to keeping your financial information away from potentially unscrupulous merchants, you should know that PayPal is not a bank, nor is it regulated like a bank. This means you are relying upon PayPal to do the right thing. Their policies covering payment disputes along with your exposure to potential losses are left to their discretion.

Because PayPal is a fact of life for many online purchases, the best course of action is to link only your credit card, and not your bank account to this service. In this way, you can still rely on the protections afforded by credit card laws, even if you act through a middleman, like PayPal.

Be forewarned, you may have to resort to denying the related charges on your credit card, before PayPal will reverse payment to a merchant.

Wire transfer

Wire transfers, at first glance, appear to be the same thing as Electronic Fund Transfer (EFT), but they use a different mechanism to move money electronically. Unlike EFTs, wire transfers are only between banks using either the Clearing House Interbank Payment System (CHIPS) or Fedwire for those banks that are members of the Federal Reserve System.

Wire transfers are generally viewed as the most secure way to electronically move money. Overwhelmingly, banks, businesses, and individuals who want to move large sums of money prefer to use wire transfers. The cost to use wire transfers is often much greater than for ETFs, but the added security can be worth the expense.

Mobile payments

Latest to the scene are mobile payments allowing customers to use their mobile phones to pay merchants without opening their wallets. Established players like Visa, MasterCard, and PayPal as well as newcomers like Google Wallet, Square, and LevelUp are racing to turn your cell phone into a payment terminal. Even Starbucks and Amazon have gotten into the game.

The vast majority of these use cell phone apps as a replacement for the traditional credit card terminal that customers formerly used to swipe their cards through. Ultimately, these mobile payment gateways use a traditional credit card or checking account as the means to complete payments. PayPal mobile uses the PayPal network, which itself is tied to a traditional credit card or bank account. Both Square and PayPal provide merchants with a card reader that they can mount on their mobile phones, thereby allowing those merchants to accept payment through their mobile phone.

The Federal Trade Commission has expressed the opinion that mobile phone payments linked to traditional credit cards and debit cards afford the same consumer protections as those traditional payment options.

However, mobile payments linked to prepaid debit cards and other non-bank cards and services do not. Further, consumer privacy protections for mobile payments are not as strong.

Summary

The increasing demand for 24/7 access to money, everywhere on the planet, has spurred a bewildering array of options. Some of these are truly innovative and useful; while, others can be a trap for the unwary. Unfortunately, laws and public policy rarely keep up with innovation, so you must be thoughtful about when and how to use these newer alternatives. In general, always choose to link newer services to your bank-issued credit card. This will ultimately afford you the strongest protections. Never link them to your checking account if you can possibly avoid it. Once money has been removed from your checking account, it is nearly impossible to get it back.

5   Credit Reports and Credit Scores

There are certain things that will always be part of your life: your date of birth, your Social Security number, the year you graduated from high school, and your credit history. Almost without exception, whenever you apply for a loan or a credit card, your credit history will factor into whether or not you will be approved and on what terms. Nowadays, your credit history is often used as a prerequisite for renting an apartment or receiving a job offer.

Your credit score can impact every part of your life.

Everything from buying a car, to future employment, to paying for college, to buying a house can hinge on your credit history. Is this fair? Probably not, but it is a fact. And because it is an integral part of modern life, you should understand how your credit history is tracked and reported. Armed with this information, you will know how to make your credit history work for you and not against you.

Credit reports

There are three major credit reporting agencies in the United States that track your credit-related information: Equifax, TransUnion, and Experian. These credit bureaus provide this credit information to credit card companies, banks, and anyone who has a need of it; so that they in turn, can evaluate how well you manage your money. While it is obvious that lenders will want this information, it may be less obvious that potential employers and landlords may want to look at it as well. A growing number of businesses now believe that how you manage your credit reflects upon how well you will perform on the job or pay your rent.

The following exhibit shows the information contained in a sample credit report provided by one of the major credit bureaus.

Table 5.1
Sample Credit Report

1.   Personal Information

Name	John Doe
Date of Birth	Dec 10, 1985
Social Security Number	123-45-6789
Current Address	910 Easy Street, Cleveland, OH 45439

2.   Accounts Summary

Acct Type	Company	Acct No.	Balance	Negative Items
Installment	Ford Motor	A1234	$20,000.00	No
Revolving	ABC Bank	123456	$1,500.00	No

3.   Inquiries

Date	Company requesting your information
5/5/2013	XYZ Credit Card Company
7/2/2013	Local Bank

4.   Negative items

Acct Type	Company	Status	Delinquency	Description
Installment	Ford Motor	Paid as agreed	30 days past due	No

Credit bureaus collect the information in each section from a variety of sources as described below.

- Personal information includes key information to positively identify you. This information is collected from credit applications you have recently submitted.

- Account information is collected by the credit bureau from various lenders and creditors, including the maximum you have borrowed, and if you have lived up to your credit terms.

- Inquiries track those businesses which have requested credit information about you. These requests may be initiated by them or you. For example, credit card companies may request this information without informing you, before they send you a credit card offer.

- Negative items include reports of delinquent payments to lenders along with information collected by the credit bureau from collection agencies, public record information from state and county courts, bankruptcies, foreclosures, tax liens, garnishments, legal suits, and judgments.

You should take the time to review your credit reports at least once each year. AnnualCreditReport.com is the only authorized source that is free by law. There, you can fill out an application to receive a report once per year from any one of the three credit bureaus. After you receive your report, you should look for unfamiliar accounts or inaccurate information. You will want to contact the credit bureau (websites for each credit bureau provide an online contact form) as soon as possible to dispute any inaccuracies you may find.

FICO credit score

A credit score is a number between 300 and 850 (the higher the better) generated by a formula developed by *FICO*, or Fair Isaac and Company. While there are other credit scoring agencies with slightly different number scales, FICO is by far the largest and most often used. Based upon a comparison of the information in your credit report to hundreds of thousands of others, the FICO software then predicts how likely you are to manage your debts responsibly. The formula includes not only your loan payment history, but also how well you have handled paying all of your bills; everything from your cell phone bill, to monthly rent payments, to utility bills can find their way into your credit report.

The FICO formula assigns a degree of importance to each type of credit information by using a percentage to arrive at a weighted average final score. To illustrate, in the hypothetical formula below, credit information A and B are said to be weighted equally because they each account for one-half of the final score.

$$A (50\%) + B (50\%) = \text{Credit Score} (100\%)$$

In the next formula, credit information C has been added resulting in a different credit weighting; however, in total they still add up to 100 percent of the credit score.

$$A (25\%) + B (25\%) + C (50\%) = \text{Credit Score} (100\%)$$

As you can see, in this second formula the weight, or importance, of A and B, which accounted for 50 percent of the final score in the first formula, has been reduced to half of their former weights, and C now makes up the other half. Credit information C is now equally important as both A and B together.

Table 5-2 shows the relative weighting for each credit component used in the FICO score. We'll look at each of these components individually.

Table 5-2
FICO Components

Component	Weighting
1. How well you pay your bills	35%
2. How much money you owe and how much you can borrow	30%
3. How long you have had credit	15%
4. Your mix of credit — revolving and installment loans	10%
5. How many credit applications you have recently made	10%
Your Total Credit Score	100%

Component 1:   Paying your bills

This is the most heavily weighted component, or the most important. It tracks how timely you have paid your bills. If your credit card payment is due on the tenth of the month and you pay it on the fifteenth or even a month later, your credit score will be negatively impacted. Your payment history for credit card payments, installment loan payments, mortgages, and even store credit accounts, like Sears and Macy's, will most certainly be included. This component scores the number of late payments, their frequency, and how recently those late payments occurred. For example, a 60-day-late payment counts against you more than a payment that is 30 days late. Moreover, a late payment last month will count against you more than a late payment a year ago.

Component 2:   Present and future borrowing

Component 2 (the next most important) scores your total amount of outstanding debt, including credit cards, car loans, installment debt, cash advances, and mortgages. The more you owe as compared with others with the same income as yourself, the lower your score will be. As an example, if you have a $30,000 loan for a car and you work at a near-minimum-wage job, you most likely will be denied further credit.

This component also takes into account the amount of credit you might use in the future. For example, credit card issuers typically place a maximum limit on the amount of money you can borrow using their card. In some cases, this limit may be quite high. You might be granted a $5,000 maximum, even though you routinely use $1,000. If you have a number of credit cards with high maximum limits, you would then have the potential to borrow $15,000, or even $20,000. This potential debt concerns lenders because they have found, through hard experience, that some of those with access to a lot of credit will eventually use all of it. This creates the very real risk that a borrower won't be able to pay it all back, even if they want to do so. This potential to borrow significant amounts of money will negatively impact your credit card score.

Component 3:   How long you have had credit

How you have managed credit in the past is a fairly reliable predictor of your future behavior. Someone who has never had credit poses a greater risk than someone who has proven that they can make their payments on time.

If you have a very limited credit history, it is even more important that you handle it responsibly.

Those who shun credit, preferring to use cash instead, will unfortunately handicap their credit score in this instance.

Component 4:   Mix of credit

This component looks at your experience with all of the various types of credit, such as revolving credit, installment debt, student loans, and mortgages. Those who have managed more of these types of debt will rank higher than those with only credit card debt, for example. Having dealt with a variety of credit has been shown to make for a more responsible borrower.

Component 5:   Number of credit applications

The more times you have applied for credit in the recent past, the lower your score for this component. Lenders believe that those who have been actively seeking more credit may be facing some immediate financial need, perhaps stemming from the loss of a job or financial setback. This component is adjusted to account for someone who may be shopping around for the best credit deal, such as a lower-interest credit card.

Credit score priorities

In terms of relative importance, components 1 and 2 account for the majority, some 65% of your total score. This only makes sense. Lenders want to lend to someone who has demonstrated that they can live up to their obligations as measured by Component 1: Paying your bills, while also assessing whether the total amount of outstanding debt might preclude them from meeting their obligations as measured by Component 2: Present and future borrowing.

What's not in your credit score

Credit scores take into account a wide range of information; however, according to FICO, they do not take into account the following.

- Your race, color, religion, national origin, sex, and marital status. U.S. law prohibits credit scoring from considering these facts, as well as any receipt of public assistance, or the exercise of any consumer right under the Consumer Credit Protection Act.

- Your age. Other types of scores may consider your age, but FICO scores don't.

- Your salary, occupation, title, employer, date employed, or employment history. Lenders may consider this information, however, as may other types of credit scoring agencies.

- Where you live.

- Any interest rate charged on a particular credit card or other account.

- Any items reported as child/family support obligations or rental agreements.

- Certain types of inquiries (requests for your credit report). The FICO score does not count "consumer-initiated" inquiries — requests you have made for your credit report, in order to check it. It also does not count "promotional inquiries," which are requests made by lenders in order to make you a "pre-approved" credit offer, or "administrative inquiries," which are requests made by lenders to review your account with them. Requests that are marked as coming from employers are not counted either.

- Any information not found in your credit report.

- Any information that is not proven to be predictive of future credit performance.

- Whether or not you are participating in credit counseling of any kind.

Taming your credit score

Credit scores are so important that there is an entire industry devoted to helping people manage them. Most of their advice can be summed up in this way.

Understand all credit terms before you borrow, and never borrow unless you are certain you can meet those terms.

Loan terms refer to how the borrowed money will be used, how it will be paid back, and the penalties should you fail to comply with those terms.

Here are some simple ways to improve your score.

- Obtain a copy of your credit report and review it for accuracy. Use the related credit bureau website to dispute any incorrect information.

- Don't apply for more credit than you need. As noted above under Component 5, this additional credit can hurt your score.

- Be sure to make payments for installment debt, credit cards, and mortgages a priority over all your other bills. Your payment history for these obligations will almost certainly end up in your credit score.

- If you have a limited credit history and are lucky enough or disciplined enough to pay cash for most of your purchases, consider obtaining a short-term bank loan instead. You can then pay it off quickly in order to better establish a record of prompt payment.

- Avoid credit counseling services. The Federal Trade Commission has a website — www.ftc.gov— with a section entitled *Credit Repair - How to Help Yourself*. Here you can find the same information that most credit counseling firms will provide with no cost to you.

Summary

Your credit score is one of your most important assets. It will follow you through your entire life. Ignoring it will cost you in terms of higher interest charges, denied credit, and even future job opportunities. The best way to get a high credit score is to understand the terms of any credit extended to you, and then to live up to those terms.

6   The Bottom Line

Although this book does not advocate the number-crunching budget and financial statement preparation found in many personal finance texts; nevertheless, you should as least be familiar with some accounting basics, as these can be a very practical way to keep your finances on track. This chapter will introduce you to two accounting reports, or statements, that will help you to keep score of your money management performance, as well as provide you wish the detailed information you will need if you want to improve your results.

Financial statement

First, let's look at the personal income statement. You may already be familiar with this report as it results in the so called "bottom line" that has become a cliché for summing up most every conversation or presentation. If you want to understand where your money goes, this tool will provide the answer. You'll definitely want to use this statement if you have a small business, or even a part-time, home business.

A personal income statement consists of two parts: income and expenses. When you subtract expenses from income, the result is your bottom line or net income. If your bottom line is negative, then you are spending more than you make. If it is positive, then you are making more than you spend. It's that simple. Following is an example of a very brief financial statement for the year 2012.

Table 6-1
2012 Personal Income Statement

Income	$30,000
Expense	29,000
Net income	$1,000

As you can readily see, this individual spent less than he or she earned, resulting in a positive bottom line of $1,000. That's $1,000 that can be added to savings, used to pay down debt, or even used to make an investment.

To make this report even more useful; however, income and expenses can be further broken out as shown in the following example.

Table 6-2
2012 Personal Income Statement

Income	
Job 1	$25,000
Job 2	5,000
Total	$30,000
Expenses	
Rent	$12,000
Car	3,000
Food	6,000
Misc.	8,000
Total	$29,000
Net Income	$1,000

With this expanded detail, you can see that this individual worked two jobs in 2012 and spent the majority of his or her income on rent. This process can be repeated until the report shows as much detail as desired. Moreover, it can be expanded to show how income and expenses change over time, either by showing the quarterly results as in Table 6-3 or monthly amounts for an entire year.

Table 6-3

2012 Personal Income Statement

	Qtr 1	Qtr 2	Qtr 3	Qtr 4	Total
Income					
Job 1	$ 6,250	$6,250	$6,250	$6,250	$25,000
Job 2	1,000	500	2,000	1,500	5,000
Total	$7,250	$6,750	$8,250	$7,750	$30,000
Expenses					
Rent	$ 3,000	$3,000	$3,000	$3,000	$12,000
Car	500	750	1,000	750	3,000
Food	1,500	1,500	1,500	1,500	6,000
Etc.	2,000	2,000	2,500	1,500	8,000
Total	$7,000	$7,250	$8,000	$6,750	$29,000
Net Income	$250	($500)	$250	$1,000	$1,000

Negative numbers are shown in ( )

One of the benefits of tracking financial information over time is that it reveals those instances, such as the second quarter above, when net income is negative. At such times this individual will have to use money from his or her savings or borrow money to cover the loss, at least until more money comes in over the subsequent quarters.

A personal income statement can provide other useful benefits, such as identifying wasteful expenditures and tracking your progress toward a financial goal. However, the focus of this chapter is on a second, even more important accounting statement, called a balance sheet, which shares many similarities with the personal income statement. It also has a bottom line, except that this bottom line represents your total wealth.

Balance sheet

A balance sheet consists of two major sections — assets and liabilities. Subtracting liabilities from assets results in your total net wealth, or net worth. A positive net worth means you own more than you owe, while a negative net worth means the opposite. These terms may be foreign to you, so here is a working definition.

Assets

Your assets consist of those things you own that can be expressed in dollars and cents. Assets are typically classified into three distinct categories:

- *Liquid Assets*: Liquid assets are those things you own that can easily be sold or turned into cash without losing value. These include all money in your checking account, money market funds, savings account, and of course cash. Certificates of deposits, or CDs, would not be included in this category because you typically incur a penalty for early withdrawal.

- *Large Assets*: Large assets include things like houses, cars, boats, artwork, and furniture. When creating a Personal Balance Sheet, make sure to use the market value of these items. Cars and houses especially will experience significant changes in value over time.

- *Investments:* Investments include bonds, stocks, CDs, mutual funds, 401(k)s, IRAs, real estate, and the like. You should record investments at their current market values as well. These assets can be distinguished from your other assets in that you purchase these primarily because you believe that they will increase, or appreciate in value over time. Generally, these assets, especially real estate, are difficult to turn into ready cash (liquid assets), without incurring losses from commissions, fees, penalties, or even adverse market conditions.

Liabilities

Liabilities are your debts expressed in dollars and cents and can be further classified into two categories.

- *Current Liabilities*: Those bills payable in the next month, such as credit card payments, car payments, and installment loan payments.

- *Long-term Liabilities:* Amounts you owe beyond the next 30 days, such as your credit card balance (as opposed to your credit card payment) or mortgage balance, for example.

Net worth

Net worth is the result of subtracting your liabilities from your assets. Once again, if you own more (assets) than you owe (liabilities), then your net worth is positive. If you owe (liabilities) more than you own (assets), then your net worth is negative.

Net worth is like the bottom line from your income statement, except this bottom line is a measure of your wealth, instead of your net income. Don't confuse the two. Your wealth is the fuel that powers your finances. With the right fuel, such as savings and stocks, you can generate income. Conversely, your income, no matter how high, will not create wealth. You can have a high income and still have low wealth. Only by accumulating or increasing the value of your assets (savings, investments, real estate, etc.) in an amount that exceeds your liabilities (credit card debt, car loans, mortgages, etc.) can you increase your wealth.

The ultimate goal of money management is to increase positive net worth.

Your net worth also measures your money management performance. If your net worth is positive and growing over time, then your finances are on the right track. How much your net worth increases, along with the rate at which it increases, is a measure of how well you are performing. If your net worth is negative and shrinking, then you are on the wrong track. The faster your net worth shrinks, the worse is your performance.

Table 6-4 shows an example of a simple balance sheet.

Table 6-4
Sample Balance Sheet Year End 2012

Assets	$10,000	Liabilities	$8,000
		Net worth	$2,000
Total	$10,000		$10,000

Based upon accounting tradition, a balance sheet does not use the same format as an income statement. Even though your net worth is the result of subtracting your liabilities from your assets, it is not shown as if it were a bottom line. Instead, net worth is grouped with your liabilities so that these two accounts when added together equal, or *balance* your assets. It's simple math, but can be confusing nonetheless. Here's another way of stating it in mathematical terms:

Instead of using this equation:

$$Assets - Liabilities = Net\ Worth$$

A balance sheet restates it this way:

$$Assets = Liabilities + Net\ Worth$$

Also worth noting is that a balance sheet looks at only one point in time. It measures where your finances stand on any given date. If on Dec 31, 2012, you had $8,000 in liabilities, then that is what goes into your balance sheet. Same applies for your assets. We'll cover more on this later, but for now just remember that the accounts listed in your balance sheet represent the balances in those accounts on the date for which your balance sheet was prepared.

There are only two ways to increase your net worth. You can either increase your assets, such as by adding to your savings, or you can reduce your liabilities, say by paying down your debt. This is very important to understand as it's easy to get lost in the arithmetic. Conversely, there are only two ways to decrease your net worth, either by decreasing your assets, such as withdrawing money from savings, or by increasing your liabilities, such as by increasing your debt.

Working together

Now let's circle back to see how your financial statement fits together with your balance sheet. As you will recall, if you spend more than your income, the bottom line in your personal income statement will be negative, in which case you have two choices. You can borrow money to make ends meet or you can withdraw money from savings, assuming you have enough in savings to cover your shortfall. Regardless of which of these two choices you make, your net worth will also be reduced — you will be less wealthy. Let's see why this is. Recall that:

$$Assets = Liabilities + Net\ Worth$$

If you withdraw money from savings, let's say $1,000, to make ends meet for the month, then your assets will be lower, which in turn means that your net worth has to be lowered by the same amount to keep the balance. Here is how it would be expressed mathematically:

$$(Assets - \$1,000) = Liabilities + (Net\ Worth - \$1,000)$$

Alternately, if you decide to borrow money instead of withdrawing it from savings, then liabilities will be increased, and again, in order to keep the balance, net worth has to be reduced by the same amount. In both cases, net worth, or your wealth, has been reduced.

Assets = (Liabilities + $1,000) + (Net Worth - $1,000)

Let's look at another example, because it's very important that you understand how a balance sheet works. Let's say at the end of the year 2012, you make $1,200 more than you spend, meaning you have a positive bottom line on your personal financial statement. You then decide to use that money to add $500 to your savings and to pay down $700 of your credit card debt.

Adding to savings means you are also adding to your assets, which in turn adds to your net worth.

(Assets + $500) = Liabilities + (Net Worth + $500)

Once again, net worth has to be adjusted by the addition of $500 to keep the equation in balance.

Reducing your credit card debt by $700 means that you are reducing your liabilities, which also increases your net worth.

Assets = (Liabilities - $700) + (Net Worth + $700)

In total, you have increased your assets by $500 and decreased your liabilities by $700, resulting in a total increase of your net worth of $1,200.

(Assets +$500) = (Liabilities - $700) + (Net Worth +$1,200)

Preparing your personal balance sheet statement

Now let's take all of what what you've learned so far and apply it. Suppose you don't want the hassle of preparing a personal financial statement, but you still want to measure how well you are managing your money. Simple. Once a year, prepare a balance sheet instead. Why? Because, while your financial statement measures only your income and expenses, your balance sheet measures the totality of your finances. If your spending is out of control, and your personal financial statement has a negative bottom line, then as you have seen from previous examples, your net worth will reflect this fact.

Suppose you want to make your finances look better by consolidating your debts into a lower-interest credit card, but you haven't reduced the total balance. Your personal financial statement will look better because you are paying less interest, but your balance sheet will not be fooled. Your wealth stays the same because there is no difference in the amount of your assets or liabilities. Likewise, if you defer your student loans or work out a lower payment schedule, once again your financial statement will improve because you lowered your payments, but your balance sheet won't change. There are many ways, as these examples suggest, to manipulate your financial statement, but there are few ways to manipulate your net worth. Ultimately, only the lasting and meaningful financial changes, both good and bad, show up in your balance sheet. This is why it is such an important tool.

In most cases, unless you have a great many assets or liabilities, you can prepare your personal balance sheet in less than 20 minutes. Most all the information you need can be found in your bank and credit card statements supplemented by a handful of online sites; such as Edmunds for estimating your car's value, as an example, or Zillow for estimating your home value. Here is a useful guide to help you find the information you need to help you get going.

Balance sheet resources

Assets

Current Assets
- Cash: money in your wallet or piggy bank

- Checking: monthly bank statement

- Savings: monthly bank statement

Large Assets
- Cars: online site like Edmunds.com

- House: use your latest property tax assessment or an online site like Zillow.com

- Jewelry: check eBay or use your actual cost

- Artwork: check gallery listings for a particular artist and type of work

- Computers, TV's, furniture: only include items with a current value over $1,000 — typically, these have very little value after they have been used.

- Investments, such as stocks, bonds, IRAs: use your monthly brokerage statement

- 401(k)s: use the latest report from your employer

- Real Estate: use your latest property tax assessment or an online site like Zillow.com

- CDs: use the face value

Liabilities

Current Liabilities

- Monthly Bills (ex. debt): include cable, cell phone, Internet, utilities, rent, food, dues, memberships, insurance premiums, etc.

- Mortgage Payment: monthly statement

- Credit Card Payment: monthly statement

- Car Payment: monthly statement

- Installment Debt: monthly statement payment amount

Long-term Liabilities

- Credit Card Debt: monthly statement balance

- Auto Loans: monthly statement balance

- Mortgage: monthly statement balance

- Installment Debt: monthly statement balance

Net worth

- Subtract Total Liabilities from Total Assets.

Other benefits of a personal balance sheet

There are a number of other useful ways you can use the information contained in your balance sheet. These rely upon comparisons, or ratios between the various components to provide you, or lenders, with insight into areas of potential concern.

Liquidity ratio

This is a simple comparison of your current assets — those assets that can be readily turned into cash — to your current liabilities, basically your monthly debt payments. If your current liabilities exceed your current assets, then as you probably already know, you won't be able to pay your bills. Most financial experts agree that you should have at least six times more in current assets than you do in current liabilities, or a liquidity ratio of 6. Why? Because the lower your liquidity ratio, the less cash resources you have to handle emergencies. At some point you won't be able to borrow any more or put off your payments. You will then have to start liquidating assets to pay your bills.

Debt ratio

Another handy ratio results from comparing your total debt to your total assets. This is a measure of your long-term financial stability. Lenders have found that the closer this ratio comes to 1.0, or in other words, the closer you get to the point where your debts equal your assets, the greater are the odds that you will be a credit risk.

At a bare minimum, you should have a ratio of 1.2 to 1, meaning your assets are worth about 20 percent more than what you owe on them.

Summary

Your balance sheet is the bottom line, so to speak, of your money management performance. If you can point to a growing, positive net worth, then your finances are heading in the right direction. If your net worth is negative or shrinking, then you are heading for a train wreck.

In the seminal work by Thomas Stanley and William Danko, *The Millionaire Next Door,* the authors champion the traits of what they called prodigious wealth creators or PAWs. These are individuals who have created high levels of wealth given what might otherwise be expected relative to their income and age. In other words, they are much wealthier than their financial peers. In fact, PAWs' net worth is double that which would be expected given their age and income. Want to test how you measure up? The authors provide a simple formula to calculate the expected wealth or net worth as follows:

Expected Net Worth =
(Age x realized, pretax, annual income) ÷ 10

For example, a 40-year-old with a net pretax income of $50,000 would have an expected net worth of (40 x 50,000) ÷ 10 = $200,000. To qualify as a PAW, they would have to have double this amount or $400,000. This then, is one wealth benchmark to shoot for.

In the end, it doesn't matter how you add to your wealth, whether it's by paying off all of your debts or maxing out your 401(k) or scoring a good run in the stock market. Wealth is wealth. The bottom line is that if you are living a fulfilling life while still increasing your net worth, then you have achieved the ultimate goal of personal finance.

7   Student Loans

Student-loan debt has fast become one of the largest sources of consumer debt, surpassing both auto and credit card debt — having nearly tripled in the last three years to almost one trillion dollars. Thirty-seven million Americans now have outstanding student loans. Here are some facts about these borrowers that may surprise you.

- 17% are older than 50
- 14% have at least one past-due student loan
- 42% are between the ages of 30 and 50
- The average loan balance is $26,600
- 10% of borrowers owe more than $54,000

Managing student debt has become the elephant in the room of personal money management. Borrowers are learning the hard way that recklessly piling on debt for a college education, without considering the realities of their future careers, is a ticket to financial disaster. Since the cost of a higher education is unlikely to become more affordable anytime soon, borrowers will have to become more savvy educational consumers, if they want to escape a lifetime of crushing student debt repayment.

Many borrowers might well have saved themselves this fate, had they followed the following three, simple guidelines.

1. Know your future job prospects.

2. Find the best educational value for your chosen career.

3. Know the student loan terms before you borrow.

Let's examine each of these in detail.

Know your future job prospects

What do you want to be when you grow up? In the past, the college years were a more forgiving time to explore this question. Not so anymore. Thanks to ever increasing competition for jobs, combined with the high cost of an advanced education, this question has been reduced to simply — can I get a well-paying job when I graduate? Sorry, philosophy majors, but it's a fact of life. Harsh reality dictates that you get a degree with job prospects, saving the soul-searching for your free time. This may strike some as callous or shallow, but the misery of student loan debt combined with low-wage employment far outweighs any angst over contemplating what might have been.

Finding reliable job information can be a hit-or-miss proposition, but thanks to pressure from the public and Congress, much more is finding its way into publicly accessible databases. In many instances, this information is reasonably comprehensive.

The National Association of Colleges and Employers, or NACE maintains an extensive website — www.jobsearchintelligence.com— that provides salary data based upon college major area of study, desired post-graduation job title, desired work location, years of education, work experience, and even college grade-point average.

Another worthwhile Internet site, www.CollegeMeasures. org, currently publishes an extensive database of salary and associated college costs by major area of study for the states of Arkansas, Tennessee, Virginia, Florida, Colorado, and Nevada, with more states slated to be added in the future. This tool allows you to directly compare starting salaries for the graduates of any public or private college within these states by chosen major along with the costs of attending these institutions. In other words, you can compare directly if graduating from a high-cost college results in a better-paying job. Many students may find that the best college deal beats the best (most expensive) college reputation.

Other states have begun efforts to post detailed job information about graduates of their higher education institutions on the websites for their respective Departments of Higher Education. The level of detail varies, but the pressure to make it more comprehensive is building.

Finally, you can always find useful information at your college or high school counseling office. However, to date these resources haven't effectively deterred students from making poor higher-educational choices.

Find the best educational value

Much like post-graduation job information, estimating how much you'll ultimately pay for a college education has been an effort in futility. College promotional booklets show only the sticker price, which most students do not pay. Financial aid letters give an incomplete picture, rarely spelling out how aid will change over four years or translate into monthly loan payments after graduation.

Fortunately, college educators in collaboration with the U.S. Department of Education are launching tools to shed light on this murky process. One of the newest is the Department of Education's College Scorecard (www.collegecost.ed.gov/scorecard). The scorecard is a nifty, interactive site where you can search by degree or major, distance education, state, school size, and campus, among other criteria, to find potential schools. The site also includes community colleges and technical schools.

Each college has its own page with five measurements of affordability and quality, including net cost (after grants and scholarships), graduation rate, loan-default rate, and median amount borrowed. (The fifth measure, data on post-college employment, is slated to be added.) Meters and charts show how each school compares with its peers, and embedded links lead to net-price calculators on each school's website.

Some college administrators are also trying to make the cost of attendance more transparent. The University of Dayton, for example, has announced that its 2013 incoming freshmen will receive a two-page "prospectus" detailing their billable expenses over four years, plus a promise that aid will increase in line with tuition.

The U.S. Department of Education and the Consumer Financial Protection Bureau have developed a standardized financial aid shopping worksheet, which has been adopted by over 600 schools as of the date of this publication. The State

University of New York, for example, has begun a pilot program using the new worksheet along with enhanced loan-counseling services at their six campuses for the 2012 school year.

A college education has to be viewed as if it were any other consumer good, no different than buying a new car or a house. Prospective buyers have to become savvy educational consumers or else risk permanently handicapping their financial futures.

Consumers who would otherwise spend weeks shopping for a new car or even a new computer rarely bother to invest the same effort toward researching college costs and student loans.

Know the loan terms before you borrow

Most students cannot avoid student debt altogether — college has become just too expensive. Given this, a prospective student loan borrower would do well to understand how these loans actually work. Many assume that a student loan is like any other loan, simply a car loan or a mortgage by a different name. Student loans are very different, and the differences can be shocking as well as financially painful for the unwary.

Let's begin with the basics. Student loans are loans either made by the federal government, called *direct loans,* or by banks and credit unions, called *private loans.* The purpose of these loans is restricted to helping students pay for college tuition, books, and living expenses. Borrowers can also use student loans to attend community college, trade, and technical schools. Some federal student loans are subsidized, in that the U.S. government pays some of the loan costs in order to provide lower interest rates and better repayment terms. You must be a U.S. citizen with a valid Social Security number to qualify for a direct loan.

Bankruptcy is no escape

Student loans belong to a select group of obligations that are very difficult to escape repaying. While most other loans can be canceled, or *discharged,* through bankruptcy, student loans are an exception. These loans can potentially remain with you for the rest of your life. Therefore, it is extremely important to understand your obligations as defined in the loan provisions, as you will most definitely be held accountable if you fail to fulfill them.

As with all debt, and especially so with student loans, the best advice is to borrow as little as possible, regardless of whether it is from the government or private lenders. You should exhaust all non-loan financial aid, including Federal Supplemental Educational Opportunity Grants, Pell Grants, TEACH Grants, Federal Work-Study, and scholarships, just to mention a few. These forms of financial aid do not require repayment; however, there are also strict requirements as to who may qualify to receive such financial assistance. In general, if you grew up in a solidly middle-class family, you will most likely not have access to these resources as they are reserved for low-income students.

For most students, student loans are their only real choice. And given this choice, you first should apply for direct loans, or federal loans, as these will generally have the lowest interest rates and the best repayment terms.

Federal student loans

According to the Consumer Finance Bureau, approximately 85% of direct student loans are made through the federal Department of Education.

Stafford loans, subsidized Stafford loans, and PLUS loans are the three most common federal loan programs.

The amounts that can be borrowed under each loan program are capped depending upon whether students are graduates or undergraduates, their year in school, and whether they are living as dependents. All direct loans offer a fixed low-interest rate and fixed payments commencing after a grace period, usually six months after graduation.

The Stafford loan and subsidized Stafford loan are made only to students, as opposed to their parents. Only low-income students with a demonstrated financial need are eligible for a subsidized Stafford loan, which is subsidized to the extent that interest charges are paid by the government while the student is in school. Stafford loans, unlike *subsidized* Stafford loans, merely defer interest payments (adding them onto the loan balance) while the student is in school. Piling up interest on top of interest greatly increases the final debt load.

A PLUS loan, or Parent Loan Undergraduate Student, is a direct loan made to parents of undergraduate students. The parents must qualify based upon an acceptable credit history and capacity to make repayment. The student must be under 24, single, and have no dependents. These loans carry a higher interest rate (currently 7.9%) than the other two direct loan programs. In addition, there is a fee (currently in the amount of 4% of principal) assessed as loan amounts are disbursed.

Repayment triggers

Contrary to what you may think, repayment can be triggered at any time, not just upon graduation. Should a student leave school or even if a student stays in school, but allows their course load to drop to half-time, they will have to begin loan repayment. If however, should either of these events occur and the student take corrective action within a six-month grace period, then repayment will again be deferred until after graduation.

Under the *standard plan*, once repayment starts, the student has ten years to repay the loan through fixed monthly payments with a minimum of at least $50 per month. There are a number of modifications available to the standard plan, which provide for more time for repayment along with a commensurate decrease in the payment amount. These modifications go by names such as Income Based Repayment, Graduated Payments, and Income Contingent Repayments. All of these modifications come at a price. Each will increase the total amount a student will ultimately have to repay, much like minimum credit card payments increase the total cost of credit card debt.

It is possible, in some very limited circumstances, to qualify for student loan cancellation, meaning students can escape paying off some of their loans. These loan-forgiveness provisions require a lengthy repayment period first (ten or more years), accompanied by continuous employment in public service or a nonprofit job. There are other cancellation options as well, but qualifying for them can be equally lengthy and difficult.

You cannot escape the consequences of default

You should understand that failure to repay a direct federal student loan, termed a *loan default*, will result in severe penalties as listed on the *Federal Student Aid* website (www.fafsa.ed.gov).

If you default:

- We will require you to immediately repay the entire unpaid amount of your loan.
- We may sue you, take all or part of your federal and state tax refunds and other federal or state payments, and/or garnish your wages so that your employer is required to send us part of your salary to pay off your loan.
- We will require you to pay reasonable collection fees and costs, plus court costs and attorney fees.
- You may be denied a professional license.
- You will lose eligibility for other federal student aid and assistance under most federal benefit programs.
- You will lose eligibility for loan deferments.
- We will report your default to national consumer reporting agencies (credit bureaus).

Loan deferment and forbearance

Provided you qualify, the government may grant a temporary halt to your payments through either a deferment or forbearance.

A deferment is a period of time, during which payments are suspended. It is granted only in special situations, such as re-enrollment in school, unemployment, military service, or economic hardship.

If you have a subsidized Stafford loan, the government will make your interest payments at no cost to you for as long as your loan is deferred.

If you can't qualify for loan deferment, you can still receive a loan *forbearance*, during which time the government will temporarily halt your payments (in one-year increments) for up to three years.

Forbearance is granted to those not qualified to receive a deferment. Forbearance provides the same payment-suspension benefits; however, interest charges continue to accrue until loan payments resume.

Regardless of whether you have a subsidized loan or other direct loan, during loan forbearance the government will not make your interest payments — all interest charges will be added onto your loan principal.

Let's look at an example of the financial consequences that can result from loan forbearance. Consider the following two cases shown in Table 7-1: *Case 1* is for a student who has an initial loan balance of $25,000 with an interest rate of 3.4%, and *Case 2* is for the same student with an interest rate of 6.8%. The former rate is the one currently in effect, while the latter is the one which is likely to go into effect in the near future. Let's also suppose that in both cases, the student has made payments for two years of a ten-year loan-repayment schedule, at which point, the student has opted for a three-year loan forbearance.

Table 7-1

	Case 1	Case 2
Interest Rate:	3.4%	6.8%
Original loan balance	$25,000	$25,000
Loan balance after 2 years (at start of forbearance)	$20,655	$21,257
Monthly loan payment amount	$246	$287
Interest added on to principal (during forbearance period)	$2,215	$4,795
Principal balance at end of forbearance period	$22,870	$ 26,052

Note that in both cases the loan balance after forbearance is greater than the balance at the beginning, owing to the interest charges accrued during the three years of forbearance — $2,215 additional interest in Case 1 and $4,795 additional interest in Case 2. Note also that the higher the loan interest rate, the more the principal balance increases. In fact, in Case 2, the deferred loan balance exceeds the original loan amount, offsetting more than two years of payments!

Loan forbearance can be a painfully expensive price to pay for short-term financial relief. You should make every effort to at least keep up your interest payments during loan forbearance, otherwise you may negate all of the payments you have made to date.

Perkins loans

Perkins loans are low-interest (currently 5%) government loans made to students with exceptional financial need. Unlike Stafford and PLUS loans, these loans are made through the financial aid office of the college or university, which also administers the loan. There are no loan fees, but there are restrictions as to the amount that can be borrowed at any given time. These loans have a grace period after graduation of nine months before payments commence. All of the cautions mentioned above regarding default, deferment, and forbearance apply equally as well to Perkins loans.

Private student loans

Private student loans resemble direct loans except they are made by banks, credit unions, and other lenders instead of the government. In order to qualify for these loans, you must have an acceptable credit history. One of the largest private lenders is Sallie Mae, a government lender recently turned private. Unlike direct student loans from the government, private lenders generally charge more fees — and higher fees — for loan modifications, such as forbearance or restructuring loan repayment terms.

As with government student loans, private student loans can be just as difficult, if not impossible to discharge in bankruptcy. Should you default, however, private lenders have fewer tools than the federal government to enforce collection.

A college education has become so expensive that many students will need a combination of private student loans on top of their government loans to pay for it all. The need to make every loan dollar count has never been greater.

Budgeting for a student loan

Before we look at a case study, you will first need one more piece of information. There is a developing consensus among financial planners as to what constitutes a reasonable amount of student loan debt, and a comfortable budget for repayment.

- The total amount borrowed for your entire degree program should not exceed your expected starting salary.

- Your monthly payments should not exceed 8% of your gross income.

These guidelines are just that — *guidelines*. You may have good reason for ignoring them, but if you do, it should be because you have made a thoughtful decision, rather than falling prey to colorful college brochures and sales pitches.

Real-world example

Let's walk through a detailed example of how you might apply the information in this chapter. Let's suppose that you or your child is a high school senior who wants to attend a four-year college in Pennsylvania with an intended major in design and visual communications (just to pick a random college and major) with the aim to get a job in graphic design in the

Pittsburgh area upon graduation.

The first thing you would do is go to one of the websites mentioned above — www.salarysearchintelligence.com for example — to research your potential job salary. The interactive tool on this site will require some pieces of information you won't have yet, such as the institution from which you graduated and your GPA. It's okay to fudge the data where you must. For example, you might pick Carnegie Mellon University and a GPA of 3.0 to 3.4 to start. Just use something plausible, all you're after is a ballpark estimate. Based upon the results from this search you find that a recent graduate working in visual arts and communications in the Pittsburgh area can expect to start out making around $32,500 a year.

Following the student-loan-budgeting guidelines, this is the maximum amount you will want to borrow for a four-year degree in design and visual communication. Using a student loan repayment calculator (www.directed.gov/calc.html) you can then see the following repayment schedules for a loan of $32,500 with an interest rate of 6.8% per year (the Stafford loan rate as of the date of this publication). Here are the various repayment plan options:

- Standard repayment at $324.01 for 120 months for a total of $44,881.33

- Extended repayment at $225.50 for 300 months for a total of $67,672.03

- Extended graduated repayment beginning at $184.17 for 300 months for a total of $73,295.54

- Extended graduated repayment beginning at $215.73

for 300 months for a total of $48,295.11

The last three graduated repayment programs will fit within the second recommended student loan guideline, which suggests that you keep your loan repayments below 8% of your starting salary, or $217.00 per month in this case.

Starting Salary ($32,500 / 12) = $2,708 / month

$2,708 x 8% = $217.00 / month loan payment budget

The only problem is that graduated repayments entail stretching repayment out for the next 25 years! A seeming lifetime of repayments.

After much soul-searching, you decide that a student loan budget of around $25,000 with 10 years of equal payments of $287.70 or about 11% of your starting salary feels like a better starting place. If you have to, you can always fall back on a greater loan amount or extended repayment after you have done your higher-ed shopping.

As a process, it's best to establish your budget first, before you go shopping. This makes you keenly aware of how expensive some of your potential educational choices really are. It's the same thinking as checking your bank balance before you make a large purchase at the shopping mall.

Armed with a budget of $25,000, you then go to the Department of Education Scorecard site,www.collegecost. ed.gov/scorecard, to see how far your student loan will stretch. On this site you can compare estimates for the four-year costs of various Pennsylvania colleges offering degrees in your prospective major. Below are the choices presented.

Table 7-2

Institution	Locale
Carnegie Mellon University	Pittsburgh
La Roche College	Pittsburgh
Lehigh University	Bethlehem
Point Park University	Pittsburgh
Robert Morris University	Moon Township
The Art Institute of Pittsburgh – online	Pittsburgh
Westminster College	New Wilmington

Next, you look up each institution to get more detail about their costs and student loan information.

Table 7-3

Institution	Net Price per Year	Median Federal Student Loan	Default rate %
Carnegie Mellon University	$32,054	$22,115	1.4
La Roche College	$18,575	$18,738	6.7
Lehigh University	$24,510	$22,125	1.9
Point Park University	$20,222	$23,103	10.0
Robert Morris University	$21,573	$22,718	4.0
The Art Inst of Pittsburgh – online	$26,617	$9,500	23.3
Westminster College	$20,533	$24,000	3.9

Here are some things to keep in mind as you digest the numbers in Table 7-3.

- These are general statistics for all students who attend these institutions.

- These are not specifically for students with any given major.

- Some institutions will attract students from affluent families who can pay more of their college expenses and therefore borrow less.

- Net price per year is the cost of college minus other forms of financial student aid for which you may or may not qualify.

- The student loan debt shown is only for federal loans, and doesn't include other private loans.

With these cautions in mind, it is a real eye-opener to realize that a bachelor's degree from Carnegie Mellon costs upwards of $128,000, while the same degree from La Roche College cost $74,000. Despite the range of costs, your budget of $25,000, as compared with the median federal loan debt indicated for each of these institutions, means that all of these colleges are plausible choices. But, there still remains the reality that $25,000 applied against the total cost of a four-year degree leaves another $103,000 that has to be covered for Carnegie Mellon or $49,000 for La Roche College.

Now it's time to go over to the NACE salary calculator (www.naceweb.org) and see whether the starting salary for graduates of Carnegie Mellon versus La Roche College justifies the added expense.

Of course, expense is not the only criteria for choosing a college. The reputation and quality of education matters most. In addition, some schools may have a stronger degree program for one major and not for another. This exercise is simply a starting point. However, it does provide a dollars and cents way to compare different degree programs based upon a financial analysis, instead of glossy brochures.

Everything else being equal, including GPA and desired work locale, graduates from La Roche College can expect a starting salary of $31,700, while graduates from Carnegie Mellon can expect a starting salary of $33,300 or a difference of $1,600 per year. In the final analysis, you'll have to decide whether it's worth an additional $54,000 to graduate from Carnegie Mellon. Based upon expected starting salaries alone, the added expense wouldn't appear to be justified.

Summary

Let's sum up what this bit of research has provided you as a college shopper.

1. The starting salary for your prospective major is $32,500.

2. Based upon recommended student loan guidelines, you can afford to make student loan payments of approximately $217.00 per month.

3. Depending upon the repayment options, you could afford to borrow up to $32,500, however in order to do that, you would have to stretch out your repayment for 25 years.

4. You have discovered that even with a lower total student loan budget of $25,000, all of the colleges in

Pennsylvania are viable options.

5. A gap still remains between what you intend to borrow and the costs you will have to cover out of pocket. The difference between the most expensive and least expensive educational alternatives for your major amounts to $54,000 over four years.

6. You have learned that the difference in the first-year annual starting salary for a job in your chosen career, based upon a degree from the least and most expensive college choices, amounts to $1,600.

7. You have real financial data to weigh in your decision, instead of promises and marketing pitches.

8. This entire effort required no more than twenty minutes to complete. Consistent with the theme of this book, a quantum return for the time invested.

This process could just as easily have been applied to other colleges in other states, which you may now want to explore for your own circumstances. You might also wish to look at other locales to begin your career, as other cities will pay more or less for someone graduating with your chosen major. These are all part of the alternatives you will want to explore before you sign away the next ten to twenty-five years of your life.

8   Buying Your Home The Right Way

Buying a home is one of the largest financial decisions you are likely to make in your lifetime. In this chapter, you will learn how to do it the right way by avoiding the mistakes others have had to learn through painful experience.

The last few years have been an eye-opener for anyone who thought that the value of real estate can only go up. Contrary to prior conventional wisdom, owning a home is not a sure bet. Just like gold, stocks, and copper, the value of your home can both increase and decrease.

But why is that? Because we live in a market economy. A market economy means that before any value can be placed on real estate (or anything else), a seller and buyer must first arrive at a mutually agreeable price. By way of contrast, countries like North Korea or Myanmar, for example, have centrally planned, or command economies, where the government sets the prices.

And, as you most likely know, buyers and sellers can disagree, sometimes wildly, about what constitutes a mutually agreeable price. The source of this disagreement can be summed up this way.

All buying decision are emotional.

This may not sit well with those who believe that they use a cold, rational process when they buy something. However, consider the following list of typical home features which must be translated into the final price. How many of these are subject to calculated, analytical thought and how many are based upon subjective, or emotional criteria?

- Views
- Privacy
- Interior finishes
- Kitchen size and décor
- Architectural style
- Quality of the neighborhood
- Floor plan

How do you use objective criteria to put a price on paint colors, tile selection, carpet, and kitchen cabinets? Ultimately, how much value to attach to such features comes down to personal taste, which is another way of saying an emotional response.

On top of these subjective criteria, buyers and sellers also factor in an expectation about the direction of future home prices. A seller who expects home prices to increase will be less willing to sell at a low price, while buyers with the same expectation will be more likely to pay a higher price.

Looking back at the last five years, most buyers expected home prices to fall. Although sellers resisted selling at low prices, prices did indeed fall. It's also true that a lot of home sellers refused to sell their homes at a low price and withdrew their houses from the market. But for those with no choice, they had to sell cheaply or not sell at all.

As of the publication date of this book, housing prices are increasing again, in some cases dramatically. Buyers' and sellers' expectations have switched yet again, and now buyers are paying more for the same houses that they wouldn't have touched only two or three years previous.

As you can see, the combination of valuing a home based upon emotional criteria along with expectations about the direction of future home prices only guarantees that prices of homes will go up, down, and sideways. Some buyers might be able to time their purchase to take advantage of this volatility; but for most, buying a home, at least a primary home, is largely motivated by lifestyle needs.

Given that you have little control over the value of your home in the future, the only practical way to approach this significant money management decision is to build in the expectation that rising home values will not rescue you from overextending your finances in the first place.

The intent of this chapter is not to show you how to buy real estate, or any other investment for that matter — there are plenty of books that cover this information in more depth. Rather, this book is about showing you how to buy a home that fits your financial means. Even though all buying decisions are emotional, that doesn't mean you should just throw up your hands, abandoning all rational constraint. With this in mind, what follows are some guidelines to keep you from buying more house than you can afford.

Never overextend your finances to buy a home.

If you buy a home beyond your means, you will have no cushion against downturns in the economy or adverse changes in your own financial situation. Should you lose your job for six months, or incur a large medical bill, or any of a hundred other financial calamities, you don't want to add losing your home on top of these. And if you do suffer financial setbacks, don't even think about walking away from your home mortgage. Those so called "strategic defaults," wherein homeowners simply ignored their obligation to make their mortgage payments, will haunt those borrowers for years to come. Everything that has been said previously about credit scores can be said about a mortgage default. Do those people really think that future employers and lenders will ignore this short-sighted, self-serving tactic?

Debt ratio

What then is considered a reasonable amount to pay for your home? The FHA, or Federal Housing Administration, which insures millions of home loans, suggests using a debt ratio as a starting point. A *ratio* is a way to compare one number to another. For instance, two-thirds of a cup of flour is a ratio. If you divide a cup into thirds, the correct amount of flour will fill up two of those thirds. Expressed as a percentage, which is just another ratio based on 100, this ratio translates into 66.7%.

A *debt ratio* is measured the same way. It is the ratio, expressed as a percentage, of the total amount of money you spend on your monthly loan payments as compared with the total amount of money you earn.

The FHA recommends 43% as a maximum debt ratio. For example, if you bring in $1,000 in a month and spend $430 on loan payments, your debt ratio is 43%. In mathematical terms, it is expressed as follows:

$$\$430 \div \$1,000 = 43\%$$

There are a number of important details to bear in mind when you calculate this ratio for yourself.

- Your income does not include money you receive from allowances and gifts. Lenders feel that this source of money cannot be depended upon in the future (nor should you).

- Income from your job should be the gross amount earned, before taxes are subtracted.

- The debt payment part of the ratio is the sum of the minimum required payments for any and all of the following: auto loans, student loans, personal loans, and credit cards.

- Payments for utility bills, car insurance, health insurance, and cell phones do not count.

You will also need to include your prospective mortgage payment as part of this debt ratio calculation, including taxes and insurance; in other words, all of the costs of owning your future home.

A debt ratio limit of 43% is not a magic number. This is the maximum limit. Beyond this, few lenders will want to lend to you. If they do, they will most likely offer onerous terms.

Bear in mind that some day you will also want to borrow money for a car, for example, and your current debt, including your mortgage, will count against you. It will limit your *debt capacity*, or your ability to borrow more money. Moreover, even if you can borrow money at an acceptable rate, you will also reduce your cushion against future financial setbacks.

Rather than pushing your mortgage to the limit, a far better alternative is to either increase your down payment, find a cheaper home, or both. Here's a sobering way to look at it: every $10,000.00 you borrow with a typical, 30-year, fixed rate mortgage, at say 4%, will cost you over $17,000 before it's all paid back. That's $17,000 that will come out of your future earnings. What else could you buy with an extra $17,000?

Suppose you are considering buying one of two homes. Both are in the same neighborhood with about the same size and layout. One home costs about $10,000 more than the other, but it has nicer carpeting, and newer appliances. In light of the true costs of borrowing, could you not in the future upgrade the cheaper house with the exact same amenities for a lot less than $17,000?

This is the way to look at any home buying decision. Don't fall into the trap of thinking only about the monthly payments. The monthly payment required to borrow that $10,000 at 4% amounts to only $48.00 — just pennies a day as the ad says. Well, those pennies will eventually add up to $17,000.

The alternative to buying a less expensive home is to increase the down payment, thereby also reducing the loan amount. In general, for your primary home, a safe guideline would be to shoot for 20% of the home price. There is yet another benefit to making a larger down payment. Mortgages with less than a 20% down payment typically include an additional monthly amount for private mortgage insurance or PMI, a surcharge that protects the lender from the higher defaults expected from borrowers with low down payments. Depending upon how much you put down, such charges can range from .5% to 1% of the loan amount per year. On a $200,000 mortgage that translates into an extra $1,000 to $2,000 per year. You probably have a lot of alternative uses for that kind of money

Of course, having a large down payment means that if you sell your home for less than you paid for it, the loss will come out of your pocket, ahead of the banks. Acknowledging that this could happen should be an additional incentive to buy a less expensive home.

Having decided on a house, hopefully one which fits within these more conservative debt guidelines, you next have to decide what type of mortgage you want. There are many options from which to choose: fixed rate loans, adjustable rate loans, balloon loans, and loans everywhere in between.

Home mortgages

Let's look at a few of the more popular choices. Fixed rate loans, meaning the payments (and interest rate) are fixed for the life of the loan, are the most traditional type of mortgage. Generally the length of the loan, or loan term, is for 15 years or 30 years. There are shorter-term loans; however, loans shorter than 10 years typically aren't set up to fully repay the initial loan principal. If they were, the monthly payments would become unreasonably high. Instead, any remaining loan principal left at the end of the loan term is recovered in one final, large payment called a balloon payment. The idea behind these loans is that the borrower will secure another loan, thereby paying off the first loan, before the balloon payment comes due.

Balloon loans often have very attractive interest rates because the lenders, freed from tying up their money for 15 to 30 years, are able to take advantage of rising future interest rates, if that should happen. In turn, the borrower assumes the risk that the next loan they take out to replace the first one may also be at a higher interest rate, or even worse, they may not be able to get a loan at all.

By the same reasoning, a 15-year, fixed rate loan carries a lower interest rate than a 30-year loan. Often the difference is about .75 to 1%. While the lower 15-year interest rate results in lower interest charges, it is more than offset by the shortened period of time in which to pay the loan back.

Table 8-1 shows the monthly payment for a 15-year, fixed rate loan versus a 30-year, fixed rate loan for the same principal amount of $100,000.

Table 8-1

	15 years	30 years
Initial loan principal	100,000	100,000
Interest rate	3.75%	4.5%
Monthly payment	$727.22	$506.68

As you can see the 15-year loan payment is over $220 more per month. So what are the benefits of choosing a shorter term loan? Besides paying off the loan sooner, the 15-year loan will incur $30,900 in interest charges, while the 30-year loan for the same amount will incur $82,406, or an additional $51,506.

There is a way to have the best of both worlds — the low payments of a 30-year, fixed rate loan combined with the option to make higher payments, thus converting that same loan into a 15-year, fixed rate loan (or any length loan term you choose). And the best part is that you don't have make any special arrangements to set it up. Unless prepayment is specifically prohibited by your lender, you can simply add any extra amount you wish to your regular monthly mortgage payment. The lender will apply this extra amount against the loan principal. Don't be fooled into paying for this option. All you have to do is include the extra amount with your regular payment and the lender is required by law to apply it towards your loan balance. (If you are in arrears on your payments or underfunded on your escrow account, the lender will apply the extra money against these first.)

The best part of this elective payment option is that you can make the smaller monthly payments or the larger one whenever you want. There are numerous loan calculators on the Internet to help you calculate the additional payment amounts you need in order to convert your 30-year, fixed rate loan into a 15-year loan, a 20-year loan, or any length loan you choose.

The downside of making additional principal payments is that you will not enjoy the lower 15-year interest rate. No matter what your principal balance, your 30-year, fixed interest rate will remain the same until your loan is paid in full. Of course, you are always free to refinance your loan, a topic which we'll cover in a bit.

Adjustable rate loans provide yet another popular alternative. These come in any number of flavors. Some start at below-market interest rates with payments that escalate every year for the first five years, finally reaching some market-based level, which then adjusts annually thereafter. Others start out at a higher rate for the first year and adjust every year thereafter, but with a lower overall interest rate. The latter results because the lender receives a market-based interest rate from the start. There is nothing wrong with these loans; however, the borrower has to accept that their loan payments will change as the loan matures, possibly to the point where they are no longer affordable.

Since the last recession we have been in an environment of extremely low interest rates. Borrowers who had chosen adjustable rate mortgages came out the big winners. The likelihood that interest rates will remain at these historical lows is unlikely. An adjustable rate loan definitely adds another layer of uncertainty on top of the inevitable swings in home values. Fixed rate loans are best if you would rather not worry about such things.

Prepayment penalty

Regardless of the type of mortgage you choose, lenders can impose a prepayment penalty, which penalizes you should you pay the mortgage off, and sometimes even if you pay down a portion of your principal. You should make every attempt to avoid loans with a prepayment penalty. The only exception might be when a lender waives significant loan settlement costs in exchange for imposing a prepayment penalty of limited duration. Generally, one to two years is an acceptable period of time depending upon the amount of loan fees they waive.

Loan fees

Loan fees, or settlement costs, are the costs a lender charges the borrower for originating (setting up and initially funding) their loan. You can save a lot of money by shopping for loans with the lowest fees — a list of typical fees is shown below. Some lenders bundle these into a single amount, which can run anywhere from 3-5% of the loan amount, while others will break out the charge for each one.

- Credit reports
- Lender's attorney
- Title search and title insurance
- Recording
- Fees for other tax services
- Application
- Origination
- Underwriting and processing
- Points
- Property inspection

- Appraisal

In addition, there are other costs and fees you will have to pay no matter where you get your loan. These are an integral part of obtaining a mortgage, and you will need to budget for them regardless.

- Prepaid interest (based on the day of the month you settle)

- Mortgage and transfer taxes (determined by your state or local taxing agency)

- Private mortgage insurance (if needed)

- Homeowner's (hazard) insurance

- Flood insurance (if needed)

- Reserve (or escrow) funds for property taxes and homeowner's insurance

For those fees in the former group, the best approach is to request an estimate up-front before you go through the bother of applying for a loan, a so-called Good Faith Estimate, or GFE. You might be surprised to find these costs can vary by thousands of dollars between different lenders. Generally, if you restrict your mortgage shopping to banks, credit unions, and savings and loans you can feel confident that choosing the lowest-cost lender will be as safe as going with the higher-cost alternative.

You may be able to negotiate certain of theses fees down. Once you have a GFE from several lenders, you will be in a better position to identify which fees to target. Keep in mind that for every $1,000 in settlement costs you can avoid adding onto your loan principal, you can save around $1,700 over the life of the loan.

Refinancing

The incentive to keep loan fees low applies as well to another money management decision that most every homeowner will have to face — when to refinance a loan. At some point in the future, after you have secured your initial mortgage, you are bound to find that interest rates for new loans have fallen below those of your loan. Sometimes it's a little bit lower, like one-half of 1% and sometimes it's much lower, like 2%, 3% or even 4%. But how do you decide when is the right time to refinance?

A good rule of thumb is that you should refinance when the cumulative reduction in your loan payments will pay back your refinancing settlement costs in approximately one year.

For example, if refinancing costs $600 in loan fees, you will need to save about $50 per month in your loan payments to pay it off in one year. Focusing on both aspects of refinancing, payment savings and loan fees, prevents you from wasting money with high-priced lenders or unprofitable refinancing. Remember, none of the savings falls into your pocket until you have recouped your loan fees. If possible, pay loan fees out of pocket as opposed to adding them onto the loan principal.

Real estate investing

Finally, should you buy a house as an investment? The answer is: it depends. Obviously there are a lot of people who have made money investing in real estate. If you have experience and the financial resources, it may work for you. For most

people though, there are better investments that don't entail
the headaches and risks of owning investment property. Just
ask anyone who bought a home to flip it in the last five years,
then you'll have an appreciation for some of the risk.

If you should decide to try your hand at real estate investing,
here are the financing realties you can expect in today's
marketplace.

1.   Owing to losses stemming from the last recession, very
     few lenders are making loans for investment property.
     This means investors have to put up cash for most all of
     the purchase price.

2.   Tying up a substantial amount of cash should require
     a substantially higher return. This means you have to
     be a shrewd buyer to get the best property at a low, low
     price to start. Do you have the knowledge and skills to
     do this?

3.   You must be prepared to stay for the long term. You are
     unlikely to enjoy high returns in the short term. More
     than likely you will have to become a landlord. Do you
     have the temperament to deal with tenants? If not, can
     you afford to pay for property management and still
     come out ahead?

These factors make home investing a daunting proposition.
Investing in real estate is hard work and risky. A weekend
investor may make money, but then again, they will invest
many weekends to accomplish it.

Summary

Owning a home is still the American dream. Only recently has it become a vehicle for quick wealth. Unfortunately, it can also be a vehicle for quick wealth destruction. But those who bought homes fifteen or twenty years ago have continued to accumulate equity. The long-term wealth-building potential of home ownership remains intact, despite the setbacks of the last recession. However, only those who buy responsibly and manage their finances with a long-term perspective will be able to enjoy the eventual rewards.

9   Retirement Planning

At one time, you might have realistically expected to find a steady job with a generous pension to see you safely through to retirement. Today, things are very different. With every passing year, an ever-growing number of private employers are defaulting on their pension obligations, with no end in sight. Even public employees have found their defined benefit plans replaced with defined contribution plans instead. The message is clear — the responsibility for retirement rests in your hands.

A great deal has been written about retirement planning. Some of it is worthwhile advice, while unfortunately, a lot is simply an infomercial urging you to sign up for this program or with that advisor with the promise to offload your retirement planning headaches onto someone else. The truth is that like death and taxes, retirement planning is inescapable. Even the most basic plan beats no plan at all as you bury your head in the financial sands of self-denial. There are very good odds that you will spend twenty or thirty years in retirement, don't you think that merits a least a little planning?

Retirement planning, in concept, isn't complex. In essence, you must replace the income from your job with income from other sources. If you can't, then you have to cut your retirement living expenses. That's pretty much it — no magic. Your financial goal, while working, is to set aside enough to fund your retirement, while striking a balance between financial sacrifice and future reward. After retirement, your financial goal switches to balancing your income and expenses so that you don't outlive your money. One thing to keep uppermost in mind, your financial options become more limited as you get closer to retirement. Any plans you make twenty or thirty years before retirement are by far the most important and longest lasting ones.

Retirement Spending

It all begins with an estimate of your future retirement spending. If you don't do this, then you have no basis upon which to formulate any meaningful financial goals. No matter how far you are from retirement, you should make some attempt at a spending estimate. Of course, there will be changes in the future, and even in retirement you can still reduce your expenses, such as by downsizing, moving to a lower-cost locale, and so on; but for many people, these are fall back options, not their first choice.

Until recently, common financial wisdom pegged retirement expenses at around 75% of pre-retirement spending. The thinking was that you would realize savings from eliminating or reducing any or all of the following:

- Work related expenses
- Child rearing expenses
- Income taxes
- Home related expenses (stemming from downsizing or paying off your mortgage)
- Saving for retirement

However, many retirees end up offsetting these savings by spending more for some or all of these items:

- Healthcare

- Travel

- Entertainment

- Student loans for their kids (or themselves)

- Long-term care

Unless you make a concerted effort to downsize your lifestyle, you should probably expect to spend about as much or perhaps a little less in retirement than you do while working, making it more realistic to expect to spend around 85% to 90% of your pre-retirement income rather than 75%. At the end of this chapter, we'll go through a detailed example of how to do this.

Once you have an estimate of your retirement expenses, you can then jump to the income side, adding up the income sources specific to your situation, and then matching income against expenses. Unless you are wealthy, there's a good chance that your future retirement expenses will exceed your future retirement income, especially if you are many years from retirement. If expenses do exceed income, then you will need to use a process termed "gap analysis" to determine either how much income you will need, or conversely how much in the way of expenses you will need to reduce, in order to close the gap. Once again, we'll explore a detailed example of how this works a little later. Before you undertake this process though, you will first want to read the following two sections.

Savings withdrawals

More than likely, even if you are lucky enough to have a pension, you will have to supplement it with other income sources, including Social Security, a 401(k), an IRA, a part-time job, and so on. Modern retirement depends upon maximizing the income from each of these sources. The most common and arguably the most important of these are your savings and Social Security. In fact, according to the Investment Company Institute, Social Security will comprise 29% of the income for even those in the highest earning quintile.

How much you need to accumulate in retirement savings hinges upon two things:

1. Your retirement spending.

2. How much income your savings will support.

These two are integrally bound together. Obviously, more spending will require more savings. Less obvious is that the rate at which you spend your savings will also determine your spending. Taking too much from savings increases your risk of outliving your money. Taking too little results in unnecessary lifestyle sacrifices.

Until recently, most financial planners agreed that retirees could safely withdraw 4% of their initial savings (the so-called 4% rule) every year with little fear of outliving their money. How retirees applied this rule varied depending upon their goals and total amount of savings. For wealthy retirees, the 4% rule meant only withdrawing the interest and dividend proceeds from their savings, leaving capital gains to build principal. By adding to principal, these retirees could then commensurately increase their income with every passing year (similar to compounding interest), and at the end leave an inheritance.

For those who weren't wealthy or were disinterested in leaving an inheritance, this strategy had some shortcomings. For these retirees, application of the 4% rule meant spending 4% of their initial savings regardless of whether they subsequently made more or less from their investments. Depending upon these investment results, they either chewed up too much savings in bad times or deprived rewarding themselves in good times.

To overcome the shortcomings of the 4% withdrawal strategy, the current thinking on savings withdrawal advises using a combination of fixed and variable withdrawal rates, such that income increases when investment returns warrant, but is sparingly reduced when investment returns are low or nonexistent. Representative of this approach is one such strategy, dubbed the Modified Required Minimum Distribution, or MRMD for short. Don't let the name put you off. This is a simple and effective savings withdrawal approach, which any retiree can implement. (The following description of MRMD is based upon a 2012 research paper published by Wei Sun of Renmin University in Beijing and Anthony Webb of the Center for Retirement Research at Boston College. While there are any number of related strategies, the authors have taken great pains to make theirs easy to understand and apply).

In an effort to simplify the application of MRMD in the real world, Renmin and Webb elected to base their minimum savings withdrawal rates on the IRS's Required Minimum Withdrawal, a percentage of assets that individuals must withdraw each year from tax-sheltered accounts such as IRAs and 401(k)s beginning at the age of 70½ years (this information is readily available from the IRS). The IRS developed their withdrawal rates based upon the joint life expectancy of a couple, of which one spouse is 10 years younger than the account holder. Of course, a competent financial planner can and should modify this basic assumption and associated withdrawal rates to fit your exact situation; however, the standard IRS rates will serve for purposes of explaining the concept. Renmin and Webb also extended the minimum withdrawal rates to encompass younger account holders aged 65, which is more useful than the age of 70½ used in the IRS table. Table 9-1 shows their modified withdrawal rates.

Table 9-1

Annual MRMD Withdrawal Rate Percentages

Age	%	Age	%	Age	%	Age	%
65	3.13	74	4.20	83	6.17	92	9.80
66	3.22	75	4.37	84	6.45	93	10.42
67	3.31	76	4.55	85	6.76	94	10.99
68	3.42	77	4.72	86	7.09	95	11.63
69	3.53	78	4.93	87	7.46	96	12.35
70	3.65	79	5.13	88	7.87	97	13.16
71	3.77	80	5.35	89	8.33	98	14.08
72	3.91	81	5.59	90	8.77.	99	14.93
73	4.05	82	5.85	91	9.26	100	15.87

When retirement savings are multiplied by these percentages (based upon the age of the oldest spouse) the result is the minimum annual amount of savings that is to be withdrawn for the year. For example, a 65-year-old account holder married to a 55-year-old spouse with $250,000 in savings would multiply their $250,000 by 3.13% (from Table 9-1) to arrive at a minimum annual withdrawal of $7,825. (The savings amount used in this calculation is the balance at the end of the previous year.)

The percentages shown in Table 9-1 represent the minimum withdrawal rate, which is the fixed portion of the MRMD strategy.

In addition to the minimum withdrawal amount, this couple can also withdraw any positive investment returns for the year, such as interest, dividends, and capital gains. This represents the variable part of the MRMD strategy. For example, suppose that this couple also saw their savings increase by $8,000, a combination of interest income of $3,000 and capital gains of $5,000 (a very conservative total investment return of 3.2%). Their total annual withdrawal for that year can likewise be increased by $8,000, bringing their total savings withdrawal to $16,807 — a definite improvement over the $10,000 allowed under the 4% rule.

The withdrawal of capital gains, interest and dividends represents the variable portion of the MRMD strategy.

Continuing the example, one year hence, for this couple now aged 66 and 56 respectively, the withdrawal percentage increases to 3.22%. Multiplying their savings of $250,000 by the next withdrawal rate of 3.22% yields a new minimum withdrawal of $8,307. If they also have positive investment returns, these can be added onto the total as before.

According to Renmin and Webb, the MRMD strategy when compared with the 4% rule and a number of other withdrawal strategies, provides a superior match between the draw down of assets and life expectancy. In other words, this strategy maximizes retiree income, without increasing the risk that they will either outlive their money or leave money that they could have used to support their lifestyle.

In summary, the MRMD withdrawal strategy offers the following benefits:

- It's easy to understand and implement.

- It has a conservative withdrawal rate that better matches life expectancies to savings. Obviously, this isn't a perfect science, since there is no way to determine how long someone might live.

- It provides the flexibility to trim withdrawals when investment performance is poor and to increase them when performance improves.

- Income increases as retirees age, thereby offsetting some of the potential for increasing costs of healthcare and long-term care.

- It provides a minimum level of income which increases over time without resorting to increasing the percentage of investments in high-risk assets like high-yield bonds or stocks.

- Retirees enjoy the rewards of superior investment performance without losing the benefit of a stable, minimum income level.

As with any plan, there are also trade-offs:

- The income stream is lowest in the beginning when retirees will most likely have a more active lifestyle — the price imposed by this strategy for insuring against outliving one's money.

- Retirees may live well beyond the actuarial life spans underlying the withdrawal projections, in which case a course correction would be necessary.

- If savings investments should lose money, the minimum income from that year will be decreased as well, which means that this strategy imposes some penalty for poor investment results.

- The goal of this strategy is to exhaust the savings during the life span of the retirees. There is no provision to leave an inheritance.

Using MRMD to set a retirement savings goal

Armed with the MRMD strategy, it is an easy math exercise to translate a desired retirement income level into a savings goal. We simply use Table 9-1 in reverse. For example, if you determine that you will need $10,000 a year from your savings at age 65, then you divide the $10,000 by the withdrawal rate for a 65-year-old retiree from Table 9-1 to arrive at the required total savings. Expressed mathematically, here is how it looks:

Desired Annual Income ÷ Withdrawal Percentage Rate = Required Total Savings

Substituting the numbers from our example into this equation yields the following result:

$10,000 ÷ 3.13% (withdrawal % from Table 9-1) = $319,489

You can check your calculations by using Table 9-1 in the normal fashion. Starting with the $319,489 result from above and multiplying it by the minimum withdrawal percentage rate of 3.13% you then arrive at an answer of $10,000. This process of using the MRMD withdrawal percentages in reverse is how we will determine a retirement savings goal in the practical application at the end of this chapter.

But before we do that, we first need to cover the other important source of retirement income.

Social Security

Social Security is much more than a simple choice between taking your benefits early or waiting for a greater amount at your full retirement age. Thanks to increasing life spans, escalating benefits over time, various filing options, and spousal benefits; your potential choices can be surprisingly complicated.

Let's begin with the basics. The minimum age that anyone can file for Social Security benefits is age 62, provided of course that they have worked in Social Security covered jobs, which includes about 97% of wage earners in the United States. The so called "full retirement age," the age at which a retiree can claim their full benefit or "primary insurance amount," increases depending upon when they were born. Those born between 1943 and 1955 reach their full retirement age at 66.

For those born between 1955 and 1960 their full retirement age gradually increases to age 67 and remains at age 67 for anyone born after 1960.

While taking benefits at age 62 (approximately 70% of retirees choose this option) puts money in your pocket sooner, the penalty for taking these early payments is a 25% reduction in the monthly benefit amount you would have received had you waited until your full retirement age.

The break-even point in terms of the total amount of money received over your lifetime is around age 77.

In other words, by age 77 you will have received about the same total number of dollars in benefits, regardless of whether you elected to start your Social Security at age 62 or waited until you reached your full retirement age. Beyond age 77, delaying the start of taking your benefits will increase your total lifetime payout. And, with ever-increasing life expectancies, that difference can be significant.

In the United States, the average life expectancy of a 60-year-old male is age 83. For a female, it's 86. By definition, half of all men and women will live longer than the average. Moreover, for married couples, there is a 50% chance that at least one of them will live until 90 and a 25% chance of surviving well into their 90s (according to the LIMRA Retirement Income Reference Book 2012).

To complicate things even more, the Social Security Administration, or SSA, offers incentives to delay filing for your benefits even when you reach your full retirement age. Every year you delay results in a benefit increase of 8% until you reach age 70 (plus cost of living increases). This compounded increase, guaranteed by the credit of the United States, can add up to a substantial sum over the lifetime of those retirees who live into their 80s and 90s.

The preponderance of Social Security financial advice is devoted to maximizing the total amount of benefits received over the lifetime of the retiree. And as you will see, the analysis can become quite complicated. In fact, we can only hope to identify the key decision parameters, as a thorough analysis tailored to the unique circumstances and goals of every retiree (and their spouse) requires running detailed scenarios best left to a professional financial planner.

But is retirement all about maximizing lifetime benefits? Many have raised the issue that there is an equally important trade-off in quality of life. After all, what good is it to have the highest income when your mobility and health are declining? The very real cost of waiting to claim benefits later in life is to do entirely without those benefits in the meantime. This aspect of the decision doesn't receive as much attention as it should, perhaps because it is harder to quantify. If you spend any time reading online comments about Social Security, this is the issue that readers raise most often. It's fine to aspire to the most benefits you can get, but not if you have to make undue sacrifice to achieve them. If you don't have an alternate source of income to draw upon when you reach age 62, the option of waiting isn't an option at all. Likewise, if you or your spouse does not expect to live beyond age 77, or you expect to lose your health and mobility sooner rather than later, then your decision is simple — take the money now. If you don't believe the government will live up to its promise to pay Social Security benefits in the far future, which isn't out of the question, you should take the money now.

You should take your benefits early if any of the following fits your situation.

1. You need the money. If you can't pay the rent or buy food, you should take your benefits as soon as possible. There is no requirement to justify your decision to the SSA.

2. You're in poor health.

3. You can invest the money and earn returns greater than 8% per year (more than the return you would get by waiting). Although this is getting harder to do, it is doable. If you have the know-how or the investment opportunities to invest your Social Security benefits at high rates of return, then you can end up with more money, even if you elect for early retirement. In essence, not taking your benefits is equivalent to investing those proceeds at a risk free rate of 7-8% backed by the credit of the U.S. If you can consistently beat this rate of return, then you shouldn't delay past the minimum age to file.

As with all government programs, Social Security entails many surprising complications, the majority of which concern spousal benefits. It is one thing to take the money and run, and quite another to deny the best possible benefits for a spouse who may be younger, or will outlive you by any number of years.

If you're single, your Social Security decision is relatively simple. You can choose between having reduced benefits now or waiting until your benefits reach an acceptable higher level up until age 70. You don't have to make any other choices.

If you're married, you have many, many permutations as the following examples will demonstrate. To begin with, your spouse can claim either their own benefit (if they worked) or part of your benefit for what amounts to a supplement, increasing their total benefit to 50% of your benefit (depending upon their age). In other words, once you decide to claim your Social Security benefits, then a spouse who is at least age 62 can choose whichever benefits — their own or the equivalent of 50% of yours — will pay him or her the most.

Likewise, when a spouse reaches full retirement age, they can again opt for 50% of your benefit as a spousal benefit, and then suspend their own benefits, thereby allowing them to escalate at 8% per year until they reach age 70. At such time, they can then switch over to their own benefits, if their own benefits are greater than the spousal benefit. On top of this, if you should die before your spouse, the surviving spouse can claim 100% of your benefits or keep theirs, whichever is greater, for as long as they live.

Confusing? You bet. Whole books and websites have been dedicated to this topic. There are financial calculators such as T. Rowe Price Social Security Benefits Evaluator (www. troweprice.com/socialsecurity), AARP's Social Security

Benefits Calculator (www.aarp.org/socialsecuritybenefits) and Maximize My Social Security.com to help you work through this complex decision. In this chapter the goal is only to touch upon the possibilities so that you can make a well considered decision.

Here are some other possible strategies. Consider a married couple, Bob and Wilma, who are both age 62. Bob's primary benefit amount is $2,000 per month and his life expectancy is 80. Wilma's full benefit based upon her work record is $700 per month and she expects to live until she is 90. If they both claim at age 62, Bob will get $1,500 per month and Wilma will get $525 per month, a 25% penalty for not waiting until their full retirement ages. When Bob dies, Wilma will get a survivor's benefit equal to 100% of Bob's benefit of $1,500 until she dies at age 90. In this instance, their lifetime benefit equals $635,000.

Now suppose that Bob waits until age 70 to claim his monthly benefits, which by then will have increased to $2,640 per month. At the same time, Wilma elects to file for her Social Security early at the reduced amount of $525 as in the first instance. Once again, when Bob dies at 80, Wilma will receive his benefits at the higher level of $2,460 until she dies at age 90. This strategy will increase their lifetime benefits to $747,000 or almost 18% more. In addition, had Wilma waited until she reached her full retirement age before taking her benefits, their lifetime total would increase yet again by $12,600, for a grand total of $759,600.

Hold on, we're not done with Bob and Wilma just yet. Social Security provides yet another opportunity to increase their combined total lifetime benefits. Bob can file for and suspend his benefits at his full retirement age of 66, while Wilma can take her own benefits until she reaches her full retirement age. She then switches to spousal benefits equaling 50% of Bob's, while suspending her own benefits, which will then increase by 8% until she reaches age 70. At age 70, Bob applies for his benefits which by then have increased to $2,460, while Wilma applies for her benefits which have also escalated to $952 per month. In total, they then receive $3,412 per month. Upon Bob's death, Wilma switches from her own benefits to Bob's survivor benefits of $2,460 per month. All totaled, their total lifetime benefits have now increased to $961,000 — a 51% increase from the very first instance in which they both elected to file for early retirement at age 62.

Once again, this lifetime income analysis is based upon living long enough to enjoy the extra money. If this is your expectation as well, here is a list of reasons to delay filing for your Social Security benefits.

1.   Every year you delay increases your annual Social Security benefit by anywhere from 7-8%.

2.   If you reach age 60 and your health is good, you can expect to live until age 83, if you're a male, and age 86, if you're a female. Remember, beyond the break-even age of 77, you will receive more in total Social Security benefits by delaying your retirement until your full retirement age.

3.   You have enough income from other sources to cover the income not received by foregoing your Social

Security income.

4. You expect to be able to enjoy the extra income in older age.

Working and Social Security

If you intend to work while receiving Social Security benefits, be aware that your earnings will impact your benefits. As of 2013, according to the SSA, if you are under full retirement age for the entire year:

1. You can earn $15,120 gross wages or net self-employment a year and not lose any benefits.

2. Beyond that level of income, SSA will then deduct $1 in benefits for every $2 earned above $15,120.

In the year you reach full retirement age:

1. You can earn $40,080 gross wages or net self-employment prior to the month you reach full retirement age and not lose any benefits.

2. Beyond that level of income, SSA will deduct $1 in benefits for every $3 earned above $40,080.

As you can see, developing a Social Security strategy can be a complex effort, weighing many options before making a choice. Adding to the pressure, your decision, once enacted, will be largely irrevocable. The best advice is to seek competent help from a financial advisor who specializes in retirement planning before you file for benefits.

Pensions and Social Security

If you work in a job with a pension — congratulations, especially if you have a government job with a defined benefit plan. You should be aware; though, if you receive a pension for work that wasn't subject to Social Security withholding, your Social Security benefits will be reduced. In 1983 congress passed the Social Security Amendments containing the Windfall Elimination Provision, or WEP. In essence, this law seeks to eliminate paying overly generous benefits, a so-called windfall, to retirees who are entitled to receive both Social Security benefits and pensions from work not subject to Social Security withholding. There are any number of formulas on the SSA website to help you calculate this offset, but the outcome remains the same. Some or all of your Social Security benefits will be eliminated, depending upon your pension income.

The retirement equation

Now, let's apply what you've learned thus far in this chapter, using a hypothetical couple, Michael aged 48 and Debbie aged 42, who are just beginning to look at their retirement planning. They are both employed and presently have savings of $100,000 in tax-free accounts — a combination of 401(k)s and IRAs.

Their first step, as discussed at the beginning of this chapter, is to estimate their present and future retirement living expenses. Realizing that retirement is still 20 years off, they know there will yet be changes, however they also know that they have already made many of their lifestyle choices, which are not likely to change. Although they plan to save money in the future by either downsizing their home or paying off their mortgage, they also want to travel more. They also plan that their healthcare costs will be going up. At present they have two children whom they expect will be out of college by the time they reach retirement. Finally, leaving an inheritance for their children is not one of their priorities (according to a recent study, only 14% of the elderly felt that they owed an inheritance to their children).

Table 9-2
Annual Living Expenses

	Current	Retired in 20 yrs
House related	$5,000	$15,000
Transportation/car	8,000	4,000
Food	12,000	6,000
Travel/entertainment	1,000	10,000
Healthcare	5,000	10,000
Retirement Savings	5,000	0
Other	8,000	8,000
Taxes	12,000	10,000
Total	$66,000	$53,000

As this rough estimate shows, Michael and Debbie are projecting that their retirement expenses will equal around 86% of their pre-retirement spending. They project that some of their expenses will go down, notably house related, and some will go up, such as healthcare. The effects of future inflation, which are not included, will affect some categories more than others. Food, travel, and healthcare are most subject to inflation, while house related, thanks to paying off the mortgage, will be less affected.

To make some allowance for inflation, Michael decides to increase their future estimated expenses bringing them equal to their present-day expenses. However, he knows that this may not be sufficient should there be long periods of high inflation in the future. As an aside, an inflation rate of 3% for twenty years means that some expenses will nearly double. However, as a starting point, Michael and Debbie estimate that in twenty years their retirement spending will pretty much equal their current spending of $66,000 per year.

Next, they look at estimating their retirement income. Here is their first cut. Michael intends to work until his full retirement age of 67 before taking Social Security benefits, while Debbie intends to start hers at age 62.

Table 9-3
Annual Income

Michael's Social Security	$12,000
Debbie's Social Security	6,000
Michael's pension	20,000
Part-time income for both	6,000
Total	$44,000

Notice that by design, this list doesn't include income from their savings. We will use gap analysis and the MRMD withdrawal rates to estimate this amount.

Their projected income of $44,000 falls short of covering their estimated expenses by an amount equal to $22,000 — this is "the gap" that they will need to fill from savings.

Now Michael consults the MRMD withdrawal Table 9-1 to calculate the savings required to fill their future income gap. According to the table, the minimum savings withdrawal percentage for an account holder aged 67 (Michael's intended retirement age) and a spouse ten years younger (Debbie is six years younger, so they will want to have a financial professional customize the withdrawal rate, but we'll use the table provided for purposes of this example) is 3.31%. Using the MRMD rate in reverse as shown below, they can back into the savings they will need to accumulate before retirement.

Desired savings income $22,000 ÷ 3.31% withdrawal rate = $664,652

As an initial estimate, this savings total may be in line with their expectations or it may be wildly optimistic. Let's look at how this meshes with their current savings and rate of savings. At present, they have $100,000 in a mix of IRAs and 401(k)s. Assuming that they can achieve a 6% return on their savings investments for the next 20 years, their present savings will grow to $320,713, provided they leave it in these tax-free accounts. This leaves approximately $343,938 that they will have to add over the next twenty years to reach the estimated goal of $664,652 in total savings.

Looking at their present spending in Table 9-2, they are

adding an additional $5,000 a year to their savings. If they continue to save at this rate while investing it at 6% in tax-free accounts, they will accumulate approximately $184,000 in twenty years. In total, their savings will then equal $527,938, leaving them with a shortfall of $160,000.

Once again, using the MRMD Table 9-1, at age 67 and a withdrawal rate of 3.31%, this shortfall translates into $5,000 per year of lost income. This is the gap in income they will have to do without if they fail to accumulate the $160,000.

At this point, Michael and Debbie can explore any number of options to address this shortfall, such as:

- Delaying retirement
- Increasing part-time income
- Reducing retirement expenses
- Increasing retirement savings
- Increasing their investment returns

All of these come with trade-offs. For example, delaying retirement may or may not be an option, but does Michael want to work longer than 67? Increasing investment returns also means increasing investment risks. Do Michael and Debbie have the temperament to live with the inevitable swings in the value of their savings? These are questions that they will need to answer as they move closer to retirement. At least, through this process of gap analysis, they can put a dollar and cents value on each potential choice.

However, there is one facet of MRMD they have failed to

consider. You will recall that the MRMD rates in Table 9-1 represent a minimum withdrawal rate, not including interest income, dividends, or capital gains from their savings. With a total savings of $504,000 at the time of retirement and an investment return of 6%, there should be many years when they would have up to $30,000 in additional income, more than enough to cover the $5,000 income gap. If they choose to use MRMD for their savings withdrawal rate, their only job is to keep their non-discretionary spending (minimum required spending) below that level covered by the income provided by the minimum withdrawal rate. If they can do this, they should be able to weather those times when investment returns from their savings are low or non-existent. If they can't, then they will have to explore the other savings options mentioned previously.

Armed with this analysis, Michael and Debbie now have a savings goal and a process to reevaluate their goal as they get closer to retirement. With twenty years left to figure it out, they have the time to make the necessary adjustments. With less time, their options begin to disappear until close to retirement, the only real options left to them are to work longer or drastically reduce expenses. As with most things in life, time can be your best friend or your worst enemy. When it comes to retirement planning, sooner is much, much better than later.

Early retirement

Finally, early retirement has become a welcome option for some and unwelcome for others. If you retire before reaching age 65, you will want to continue to add to your savings, if at all possible. If you stop and think about it, there is no penalty for early retirement, if you can continue to build your savings as you did when you were working. This may not be possible for many, but if you already have substantial savings and you can continue to increase it, there is nothing to prevent you from enjoying early retirement. Balancing your spending and income while adequately building your net worth is the ultimate measure of any financial strategy.

Summary

Retirement planning doesn't have to be complex, provided you break it down into the three steps covered in this chapter:

- Project your retirement spending.
- Project your retirement income.
- Use gap analyses to formulate a savings goal to bring these in line.

When you get closer to retirement, you will want to fully understand your Social Security options so that you can also maximize this vital source of income, both for yourself and your spouse.

Finally, start early with a plan. Don't let retirement happen to you, make it happen for you.

10   Investor Psychology

It's a fact of modern life — if you want a carefree retirement, you will have to fund most of it yourself. And, like it or not, the stock market is one of the few ways that the average investor can accumulate the wealth necessary to do just that.

Of course, you can make money by investing in things other than stocks. However, if you lack the skills and temperament to invest in these alternatives, you may end up making even riskier bets with less reward in the end. Just ask those who thought real estate flipping was a path to riches. Or maybe investing in gold was a sure bet. In comparison, stocks can look like a pretty good option.

You might be wondering why this chapter on investor psychology precedes *Chapter 11 Investing Like the Pros*. Consider the results from just one of many studies of individual investor performance. According to the Wall Street research firm Dalbar, Inc., over the twenty-year period ending December 31, 2010, the average return for the S&P 500 was 9.14%, while the average return for the average individual equity fund investor during this same time period was a paltry 3.27%, a stunning 64% performance shortfall. It would seem that most individual investors make exactly the wrong choice at the wrong time. Greed takes over when caution is warranted, followed by fear, when boldness would win the day. This would seem to be the plight of the individual investor.

Warren Buffett, arguably the most famous and richest investor of our time, once stated, "Success in investing doesn't correlate with I.Q. once you're above the level of 25. Once you have ordinary intelligence, what you need is the temperament to control the urges that get other people into trouble in investing."

Temperament is another way of saying your emotions. If you can't tame your emotions, then mastery of the technical details won't help your investment performance. Surprised? You mean it's not about P/E ratios, cash flow statements, and 200-day moving averages?

You might ask if this overwhelming urge to do the wrong thing at the wrong time simply means that the non-professional isn't equipped to successfully invest in the stock market, or that the system is rigged, or even that investing in equities (the stock market) is just incomprehensible? And though all of this is true at times, unfortunately your other investment choices are even worse.

Playing it safe is simply not an option. Should you place your money into supposedly ultra-safe investments, like savings accounts and CDs, just check out your account value after a year of enjoying returns of one-half of one percent — that amounts to a whopping $50 from a $10,000 investment. Think gold is the way to go? Sure, it shot up nearly 46% in the last five years, but it also plummeted 21% in the first six months of 2013. Great for those that bought early; a tragedy for those that bought late. Real estate? We all know the story there.

If you have the training and education that affords you insight into alternative investments, then those can make sense for your particular situation. For the rest of us, if you want any chance of keeping up with inflation and building real wealth, you are stuck with investing in stocks, which encompasses a wide range of choices, including not only stocks of individual companies, but also mutual funds, ETFs, sector funds, and index funds, just to mention a few of the most popular choices.

The premise of this chapter is simply this:

Successful stock market investing begins and ends with avoiding dumb mistakes.

Behavioral Finance

Thanks to recent insights from the fields of psychology and investing, an area of study called behavioral economics or behavioral finance, there is a great deal of information about investor psychology and more importantly, strategies to replace financially dumb behavior with financially savvy behavior.

Bear in mind that dumb financial behavior does not mean that such behavior is insane or irrational, just counterproductive to successful investing. In his recent, best-selling book *Thinking, Fast and Slow* author Daniel Kahneman, a psychologist by training and Nobel Prize laureate in economics, tells us that we, as humans, have two minds: one that is quick and intuitive (System 1), and one that is deliberative and rational (System 2). According to Kahneman, we rely on System 1 more often than not, and that's what gets us into trouble.

The intuitive mind (System 1) is the emotional, gut-feeling mind, the one that sweeps us up in irrational feelings.

Intuitive decisions, as far as stock market investing is concerned, consistently lead to poor investment performance. The intuitive mind, according to Kahneman, is hard to override because we feel so strongly that its assessment of any given situation is the correct one. To make matters worse, emotionally charged, snap-investment decisions can occasionally work out, only reinforcing the problem.

In the long term, rational investment decisions, a product of deliberation (System 2), will win the day. That's why professional investment results are superior to those of the amateur investor. It's not that they were born that way, rather, through training and discipline, they are aware of their irrational, intuitive instincts and have developed ways to cope with them.

As the research results from behavioral economics and behavioral finance have become more mainstream, the sheer volume of work has become something of an ordeal to wade through. A listing of so-called cognitive biases, or systemic deviations from a standard of rationality (good judgment), runs to over 150 entries, which are further categorized into decision-making biases, belief biases, behavioral biases, social biases, and memory errors. Moreover, some biases show up in multiple categories.

With the understanding that behavioral finance research is continuing to evolve, let's dive into some of the most commonly accepted biases; the ones that most often get investors into trouble. In some cases, understanding the impact of these biases on your investing behavior is enough to avoid them, while for others, you will need a system, much

like the professionals, to keep yourself from getting in your
own way

The disinclination to save

Failing to save for retirement (assuming you have the
necessary funds) results from a disconnect between our
current and future selves. According to a prominent
research paper published by Hal E. Hershfield (Stern School
of Business, New York University) and Daniel Goldstein
(London Business School), "saving for retirement may feel to
the present self like giving money to a stranger, years in the
future." The present self feels deprived of enjoying the benefits
of his or her income, and all for the benefit of some old guy or
gal that will certainly never be them. Although the present self
knows in a rational way that they will eventually become that
future self, the intuitive mind fights for its present rights by
asserting that "you only go around once," "life is to be lived,"
and even "I may never live that long." The problem is, if you've
read the previous chapter on Social Security, you probably will
live that long, and most probably, quite a bit longer.

One means to bridge the gap is to trick the intuitive mind into
building a relationship with the future self. Seeing your older
self as real, and the impact of today's decisions on that future
self as real, is the desired outcome. Some brokerage firms have
gone so far as to create software that ages the investor who
then expresses their feelings as to how well the present self
has provided for them. Another technique is to look back at
yourself ten years ago and think about the sacrifices you made
then that your present self now enjoys — things like getting a
college education, paying off a large debt, working hard for a

job promotion, or mastering a new skill. What if your past self had simply lived it up instead? A sobering thought for many.

Loss aversion

People are hard-wired to overwhelmingly forgo the pleasure from gains in order to avoid the regret from losses. Some studies indicate that the psychological pressure from a loss is as much as twice that from a gain. This single factor has led to some of the most destructive investment tendencies exhibited by individual investors. Loss aversion creeps into investment decisions in all kinds of insidious ways. For example, some investors will sell their winners too soon in order to avoid the pain from potential future setbacks. Or they will hold on to losers too long in an effort to "at least get back to even," thereby avoiding the pain of losing money. As long as they hold on to their investment, there is hope, while once they sell, they are forced to accept defeat.

Regret is yet another face of loss aversion. Strangely, this fear of loss can compel investors to actually increase their appetite for risky investments. Suppose you have a friend who recommends a stock which subsequently goes up 50% in six months. Having failed to take advantage of this investment opportunity, you are naturally regretful and feel the pain of having lost the potential to make this outsize return on your money. The next time your friend recommends a stock, you will be more inclined to take his recommendation at face value so as to avoid another round of regret, even though you may feel less than enthusiastic about his stock pick.

The professionals handle loss aversion by establishing

formalized sell programs that leave them no alternative
for emotional denial, but instead force them acknowledge
and rid themselves of losers as soon as possible. One such
methodology is to force the sale of a less desirable investment,
a loser, as a means to raise money to invest in a new winner.
Professionals also do a lot of research so that they have
confidence in their investments, helping to counter the pain
when those investments inevitably suffer setbacks.

For most individual investors, these strategies probably
require too much effort and discipline. A far easier approach
is to simply set up an automatic investment program, thereby
removing the need to make any decisions, some of which will
inevitably led to feelings of regret. This investment strategy,
which spreads out an investment across a period of time,
investing $100 per month for twelve months, for example,
as opposed to investing $1,200 in one lump sum. This makes
it harder to determine which investment actually lost money
and by how much. Automatic investing also reinforces
desirable investment behavior — buying when the value of a
targeted investment drops, while avoiding the trap of getting
caught up in emotions, and then buying an outsize portion
just as the market tops out.

It's a little bit more difficult to rid ourselves of the
tendency to hold onto our losers too long. You might try
pairing your investment buying and selling as mentioned
above or try eliminating one loser every quarter or even
once per year so that you spread out the pain. This bias is
one of the most difficult to overcome and separates the
professionals from the amateurs.

Investment rules such as these can help free you from the pain of regret. Psychologically you can console yourself that you were only following the rules, it wasn't your fault.

Overconfidence and self-handicapping

These biases represent opposite sides of the same coin. Just as in the fictional Lake Wobegon, we all believe that we possess above-average capabilities and intellect. However, studies have shown that while we think we are right 90% of the time, in actuality it is closer to 70%. Overconfidence leads to over-trading, which in turn runs up commissions, taxes, and losses. These frictional losses can seriously dampen investment returns.

On the flip side, self-handicapping allows us to explain away possible poor performance with a convenient excuse. We might say we're feeling under the weather before a presentation, so that we can avoid the pain of failure should the presentation not go well. Self-handicapping is a way to cope with low self-confidence, which can lead investors to avoid having to make any investment at all.

These twin biases are so strong that they are often blinding to those who have them to any extent. They are deep-seated and permeate not only our investment behavior, but also our general life outlook. Once again, a planned investment program formulated in a calm, rational atmosphere, free of fear and regret, is one way to deal with these.

For the overconfident, a plan can eliminate over-trading and extreme risk taking. For example, someone who has suffered poor performance results from overconfidence might place

90% of their money in long-term, lower-risk investments like index funds, and keep 10% for high-risk investments where they are free to demonstrate their incredible investment acumen to their heart's content. And should that not prove to be the case, they won't destroy their portfolio in the process.

For those with low self-confidence, a structured investment plan can remove the need to psych up for every investment decision. An automatic investing plan, for example, requires only that you psych up once to start the program. From there on out, it's automatic. Employers have discovered the value of this preprogrammed approach in motivating employees to invest in company 401(k) plans. By simply switching from a policy that requires employees to voluntarily opt into their plans to a policy that requires them to opt out instead, these firms are reporting participation rates rising from 50% to nearly 90%, yet again, validating the power of momentum and automatic investing.

Keeping perspective

The best investing perspective is to accept that success requires a long-term perspective. Some investors will start in their twenties, saving all of their investment proceeds for retirement in their sixties. Even those in their fifties still have to keep a perspective of ten or more years in the future. Why then do we fixate on today's 100-point drop in the Dow?

Any number of psychological biases can explain this short-term focus — loss aversion, focusing effect, negativity bias, and so on — but there are also larger forces at work. Much of the financial industry is dedicated to stroking these biases to their benefit. Financial advisors, brokers, and even the media all pile on in an effort to convince you that what happens this week is more important than what happens in the next ten years.

The media has become a negativity-bias machine par excellence. Next time the market makes a dramatic move up or down, notice the vocabulary the media chooses to describe such occurrences. Stock market moves downward are described using such inflammatory terms as plummeted, crashed, and wiped out; while upward moves are described in more benign terms, such as gained, climbed, rose, and increased. It's no wonder we go around wringing our hands with worry and despair over our investments. You will always hear that stocks rose, but (there's always a "but"), they will likely fall again. Seldom or never will you hear that stocks fell, but that they will likely rise again. Instead, the media prefers to say that stocks fell; and they will likely keep falling.

Why this negativity bias has infused our media is a subject of debate. However, its impact on the individual investor psyche is not. Thinking that you are shoveling your hard-earned savings into an investment black hole can unnerve anyone. The problem is that this negative slant provides no beneficial information for you as an investor. It only serves to keeps you from investing in the one thing that will most likely provide you with the substantial wealth required for retirement.

You can combat this barrage of negativity in two ways. First, recognize how prevalent it is, and for the long-term investor, how nearly meaningless it is as well.. What will a 100-point fall in the DOW Index mean in a month? In a year? Will you even remember it at all? Since 1928 the long-term return from the stock market, including dividends, is around 10%. Even adjusting for inflation, this return still amounts to an annual 6.2%. How about bonds — a seemingly much safer alternative? Here the story isn't so pretty, returning a mere 1.8% after inflation. Or how about the stock market returns over the last 20 years, a period that includes the fierce stock downturn in 2008, the so called Great Recession? Table 10-1 shows the average and worst performance for a number of investments during that time period.

Table 10-1
20-year Stock Market Returns 1992-2012

	Avg Return	Worst Month
Mid cap stocks	13%	-42
Large stocks	11	-37
Small stocks	10	-36
Foreign stocks	10	-46
Bonds TIPS	8	0
Long-term bonds	8	-2
Intermediate	7	-2
Short-term bonds	6	1

As you can see, the stock market returns, despite the economic meltdown, as represented by mid cap, large, small, and foreign stocks, still managed to beat all of the other "safer investment alternatives" — rewarding those with a long-term perspective and punishing those lacking it (as reflected in the worst-month returns). In fact, with the proliferation of ultra-high speed trading and hedge fund manipulations, long-term investing has become the only game you can hope to win. No matter what antics short-term investors engage in, in the long term, the stock market accurately reflects the value of the underlying businesses. Ultimately, the profitability of those businesses dictates their stock price, not high-speed trading.

How do you turn off the incessant negative chatter? Here are some suggestions.

- Ignore anyone who forecasts the direction of the stock market or the economy. If they really knew, they wouldn't be talking about it. This applies doubly for professors and reporters. How about the stock market experts? According to a recent study by the Hulbert Financial Digest, market forecasts of the top 25 well-known stock market gurus on average did no better than a flip of a coin.

- Pay attention to the businesses underlying the stocks. If they are profitable, their stock will reflect that value over the long haul. Remember, stocks represent the ownership of the business. If the value of the stock stays too low for too long, someone will ante up and pay for what it's worth.

- Don't look at your investments after a sharp drop. You don't want to sell at the bottom anyway, so why rub your face in it? Wait for the inevitable rebound, even if it takes six months or longer. The damage has already been done. Had you wanted to sell, you should have done so before the drop, not afterwards.

- Stay focused on the long term. Will any news, short of a company bankruptcy, matter in a year? In five years?

This is even easier if you invest in broad-based index funds where your investment is spread over many businesses, greatly reducing the impact of the few that will inevitably fail. (See the section on diversification in the following chapter.)

- One glance at Table 10.1 above shows that even the best long-term investments have very bad months. Accept this as gospel. The better the return, the greater the risk for setbacks. This is the price of playing this game.

- Only look at your investment performance over the last three or five years. If you have invested in individual stocks over that period of time, and your performance is worse than an equivalent index average, only then should you take action to improve your investing game, or just settle for investing in an index fund.

Herding and hindsight error

Investors are bombarded with investment ideas. Brokers, television, web sites, financial analysts — all competing to convince you to buy something. Unfortunately, they often end up climbing on the latest investment to catch the public's eye, just as it tops out. Not long before publishing this book, Apple was considered a no-lose investment. Every stock guru and broker was recommending it. And for a brief period of time, it did shoot up to make it the most valuable company on earth, at least as measured by its total stock market value. A few short months later, it fell by over 50%.

Those who bought in near the top paid a painful price for this dynamic duo of biases, herding and hindsight error. Herding, or the bias to follow everyone else, usually kicks in just as a stock has reached its peak. Hindsight error reinforces this behavior by convincing investors that whatever happened in the past to rocket the stock higher will occur again in the future.

As a general rule, if a stock shows up on everyone's buy list, it has probably become more expensive than it's worth. It may be possible to make money, but it's more likely that the next move will be down. You should make doubly sure you understand why you're buying a hot investment and not just going along with the herd.

Summary

In this chapter, we've touched upon a few of the psychological errors that handicap individual investors. Above all, remember that investing is not about satisfying your emotional needs. If you get a rush from jumping into a hot investment or you are paralyzed from fear, you are working from your intuitive mind and not your reflective, rational mind. Investing can be a sane and rational process, but only if you do it with a sane and rational mindset. Successful investing comes from recognizing that your taming your emotions is the first priority for sound investing.

11   Invest Like the Pros

This is how typical individual investors behave. When the economy is good and the stock market soars, they jump into almost any investment they come across, lured by the promise of high returns and low risk. When the stock market reverses, these same investors take their inevitable losses, stash their cash in the bank, and swear to never act so rashly again. At present, stocks and real estate are beginning to get investors' attention again after five years of wandering in the financial wilderness. Now many of those who swore off these same investments are thinking maybe, just maybe they should try them again. Meanwhile, global stocks, are still on everyone's avoid list, even though some of these may be an exceptional investment opportunity.

What's wrong with this picture? Simple. Investors, claiming to be in it for the long term, are too often swayed by short-term events. Their aversion to loss, aided by the negative spin generated by the media, proves just too strong to resist. They buy at the top after the easy money has been made, then sell at the bottom, just before things turn up.

Some of them ask: why bother? After all, isn't investing in the stock market a rigged game? Why not find a job with a nice pension — put some money away in a nice, safe bank account? Right?

Wrong.

If you think you can escape this seeming madness, you might want to reassess your thinking. As you know from reading

Chapter 9, defined benefit pensions, those paying a lifetime annuity, are fast disappearing. From 1980 to 2008, the proportion of private wage and salary employees participating in defined benefit pension plans fell from 38% to 20% (according to the Bureau of Labor Statistics). In 2008, the Government Accounting Office found that of those private single employers offering a defined benefit pension, 23% had completely frozen their plan benefits with no future benefit accruals possible, and 22% had frozen either the years of service or the salary pension base.

At the same time, defined contribution pension plans, an investment account established and often subsidized by the employer, yet managed by the employee, have increased from 8% to 31%. In other words, individuals can no longer escape the responsibility of managing the investments that will help pay for their future retirement.

Moreover, even if you should be lucky enough to have a defined benefit pension, you will most likely want to supplement it with your savings. Investing in a bank account paying one-half of 1% means that you lose ground with every passing year. Even a modest inflation rate of just 3% will shrink the purchasing power of a $10,000 savings account to $7,440 in just 10 years. That's hardly a recipe for a carefree retirement.

Lastly, the longer you wait to make investments that provide higher rates of return, such as stocks, the greater the penalty you'll pay. Look at the table below. It shows the growth of $10,000 based upon an average after-tax return for stocks of 6.8% and bonds at 1.8%. (These are long-term averages dating from 1928 to the present.)

Table 11-1
Long-term Investment Returns

Years	Stocks	Bonds	Difference
5	$14,036	$10,941	$3,095
10	$19,701	$11,971	$7,730
20	$38,813	$14,329	$24,484

The cost of investing in bonds rather than stocks can amount to a whopping $24,484 penalty over a 20-year period — a 63% shortfall in ultimate value.

Need more convincing?

Stock market investors have never lost money over any 20-year period going all the way back to 1900.

A positive long-term, after-tax return of 6.8% combined with a long history of never losing money, certainly makes a strong case for including equities in your mix of investments.

Your investment mix

But, what investments should you make and in what proportion or mix? In financial planning lingo, the mix of investments is called *asset allocation*. In this instance, assets refers to stocks, bonds, real estate, CDs, bank savings accounts, annuities, municipal bonds, and essentially anything held for investment purposes.

Asset allocation

There are as many asset allocation strategies as there are

brokers, financial planners, financial bloggers, and advice columnists. Even dipping your toe into this sea of advice can be treacherous, as every strategy carries both upside promise and downside risk.

However, consistent with the theme of this book, if you understand the key hows and whys of investing, you will be empowered to navigate this smorgasbord of investment choices. In addition, the one principle you must grasp, if you want to be a successful investor, is that all of your investments, collectively called your portfolio, must work together as a whole. Creating a hodgepodge of investments, picking whatever comes along, is the very first mistake you want to avoid.

Let's look at some of the time tested investment principles and guidelines for building your own portfolio. These will constitute your investment foundation regardless of your choice of investment assets.

Risk

Everything in life has risk — everything. In this world, there are no real 100% guarantees, no risk-free alternatives. Hiding from risk, such as relying on others to guarantee your investments, is not dispensing with risk. It is only shifting the risk from the investment itself to the guarantor. That guaranteed lifetime annuity is only as good as the financial health of the insurance company that sold it to you.

The corollary of shifting risk to someone else, like a bank or an insurance company, is that you, in turn, will receive a smaller portion of the investment return. As an example, in the case of a bank CD, your portion of that return is so meager (presently .5%) that it is hardly worthwhile to even own this investment, while the bank lends that same money out at 8%, 10% and 12%. To make matters worse (as we learned in the last recession), banks can and do fail, once again demonstrating that nothing is truely risk-free.

Sometimes the risk is more subtle. If you invest in a bank savings account, for example, your main risk lies not in losing your investment, but in losing its purchasing power as a result of inflation. As previously discussed, not keeping up with inflation means that the value of your investments seeps away with every passing year.

The moral? Don't try to avoid risk. You can't. It's a fantasy. And, it some cases, it can turn into a very expensive fantasy. The trick is to understand your risks and insist on receiving commensurate compensation for them. When it comes to investing, there is only one proven way to decrease risk (but not eliminate it), and that is the topic of the next section.

Diversification

Diversification follows the old saw of "not putting all of your eggs in one basket." As an illustration of this powerful principle, let's say you decide to invest your savings in an airline stock. Immediately after you do this, the airline pilots decide to go on strike for an indefinite period of time. Your airline stock immediately tanks, and you lose half of your investment overnight. Now suppose that instead of putting all of your savings into airline stock, you had instead invested only half, and the other half you placed in railroad stock. Now when the airline pilots go on strike, you will lose 50% of your airline stock investment, but because it represents only half of your savings investment, your losses will be limited to 25% instead of 50%. By this one move, you have cut your losses by half. Each investment by itself remains just as risky; however, diversification has reduced the collective, or portfolio risk by one half.

Adding even more stocks, such as energy stocks, pharmaceutical stocks, retail stocks, and so on further decreases your portfolio risk. Every time you spread your investment over another stock in an unrelated industry, you lower the risk of loss should there be a specific event, such as an airline strike.

You can continue this process until you reach a point of diminishing returns; at which point, you will then have too many investments to manage. Your commission costs will increase as you buy and sell more securities, while eventually, some portion of your portfolio will become correlated, meaning that the risk and returns of some investments will mirror one another. For example, an investment in a hotel stock would share some of the downside risk of an airline stock, since they are both in the travel industry.

This idea of non-correlated returns (the value of any given asset moves independently of another) is the core principle of diversification. Professional money managers search for every conceivable asset category, or asset class, which can bring an additional level of non-correlated risk and return. These assets can range from the mundane of stocks, bonds, and real estate to the exotic, such as interest rate swaps, artwork, and currency futures.

Taking this idea one step further, even though investments in far-ranging stocks like airlines and pharmaceuticals will add diversification to your portfolio; these still represent an investment in stocks, an asset category which shares correlated returns for stocks in general, as in a bear or bull market.

Chasing diverse and exotic investments that maximize non-correlated returns is a pursuit best left to professionals, as these investments also introduce other risks for the unwary. Instead, let's look at the dramatic benefits you can achieve from a very limited set of three commonplace asset classes

Diversification: a simple set of asset classes

1. Stocks: equities or shares of U.S. based companies encompassing everything from large multinationals like Exxon or Apple to the smallest high-tech company, provided its stock is publicly traded.

2. Bonds: debt securities that pay the holder a set amount of interest, periodically or at maturity, as well as the return of principal when the security matures. These securities, generally called bonds, tend to have lower volatility than equities because companies prioritize interest payments over other capital obligations. In addition, the United States guarantees the full payment of interest and principal of U.S. bonds and treasury bills.

3. Cash: includes cash and money market securities, which are debt securities that are extremely liquid investments with maturities of less than one year. Treasury bills (T-bills)

make up the majority of these type of securities.

Let's look how using a simple diversification strategy employing just these three asset classes would have faired over the most recent great recession. The *All Cash* portfolio represents a $100,000 investment in 30-day T-bills. The *Diversified* portfolio represents a $100,000 investment in a mix of 70% stocks, 25% bonds, and 5% T-bills, and the *All Stock* portfolio represents a $100,000 investment exclusively in stocks.

Table 11-2

	Bear Market Jan 08 - Feb 09	Recovery Mar 09 - Apr 11	Start to Finish Jan 08 - Mar 12
All Cash	1.6%	.2%	1.9%
Diversified	-34%	63.8%	11.8%
All Stock	-48.4%	99.6%	7.4%

Source: Based upon historical monthly performance as reported by Morningstar/ Ibbotson Associates. Stock, bonds and short-term investments are represented by the DJ Wilshire 5000 index, Barclays Capital Global Aggregate Bond Index, and U.S. 30-day T-bills respectively.

As you can see, the *Diversified* portfolio not only fell less than the *All Stock* portfolio in the bear market, it ended up besting all of the others from start to finish. Such long-term performance results from both avoiding losing money in the bad times combined with capturing higher returns in the good times. If the subsequent economic recovery continues for an extended period of time, the *All Stock* portfolio will ultimately come out ahead. However, when the next bear market arrives, and it will eventually, the *Diversified* portfolio won't lose as much and the cycle will start over again. Some *All Stock* investors will accept the larger losses in the bear markets, in order to capture the higher returns afterward. Others, the majority quite probably, will see the *Diversified* portfolio as an acceptable trade-off of risk and reward.

The composition of the Diversified portfolio itself can be further tailored to suit the temperament of investors ranging from the aggressive investor, who values returns over risk, to the conservative investor, who prefer less risk at the expense of total returns.

Table 11-3
Modified Diversified Portfolio Options

	Bonds %	Stock%	Cash %
Conservative	70-75	15-20	5-15
Moderately Conservative	55-60	35-40	5-10
Moderately Aggressive	50-55	35-40	5-10
Aggressive	20-25	65-70	5-10

The world of investment choices

Your choice of assets for diversification purposes is nearly limitless. Within equities alone, you can choose from large capitalization stocks, mid-capitalization stocks, small capitalization stocks, international stocks, emerging market stocks, ETFs, and mutual funds, just to mention a few.

Beyond matching your risk tolerance, your investment in

each of these assets will also hinge upon your how soon you may need to convert some of your investments to cash (your investment horizon). Obviously, if you think you will need some portion of the your investments in the near future (a short investment horizon), you will want to limit your investment in assets like equities where you run the risk that you may have to cash out in the middle of a bear market. Likewise as you get older, your investment horizon decreases as you run out of time for your investments to recover from losses.

Maintaining portfolio diversification

Even though you start out with your ideal asset allocation, it is important to conduct periodic portfolio reviews as the value of the various assets within your portfolio will change, thereby affecting the mix. For example, if you start with a moderately conservative portfolio, the value of the equity portion may increase significantly during a bull market, moving your portfolio closer to that of an aggressive investor.

To reset your portfolio back to your ideal mix, you need to rebalance your portfolio. Rebalancing is the process of selling portions of your portfolio that have increased in value, and then using those funds to purchase other assets that have declined slightly or increased at a lesser rate. Rebalancing is another structured way to avoid the feelings of fear and greed which can lead to emotional, rather than rational investment decisions.

This process of rebalancing is part and parcel of diversification. If you don't engage in some periodic rebalancing, you will not enjoy the full benefits of diversification.

Financial scams

If you have ever watched an episode of *American Greed* on CNBC, you can't help but be struck by the unbelievable naiveté of the victims. Often you will read about scams aimed at those in desperate need of money, but the real tragedy are those who have a sizable nest egg, yet willingly jump at the chance to hand their money over to a scam artist promising fantastic rates of return.

As you read in the last chapter, every one of us is wired such that our emotional, reactive mind often overpowers our rational, thoughtful mind. Financial scam artists are masters at exploiting this cognitive bias as they play off your feelings of guilt, envy, greed, and regret.

By far the easiest way to avoid becoming a victim is to simply never put yourself in a position to be victimized in the first place. Avoiding a scam is much easier than the hard work of investigating and analyzing such opportunities. Few investors are equipped to fully ascertain the legitimacy of a financial investment opportunity, including an honest assessment of the key sponsors.

The following guidance may seem extreme to some. Some investors have willingly abandoned all such constraints, and still made money. However, just like lotto winners, you will hear endlessly about the few that scored big and very little about the multitude that didn't.

1. Don't do business with friends, acquaintances, or

relatives. Unless you're an investment professional and your friend is an investment professional, this is typically a recipe for regret. In most cases, if the investment opportunity is legitimate, raising money from friends and relatives is a last resort from the sponsor's perspective. If they could have found a well-heeled professional investor, they would have done so in a heartbeat, foregoing the hassles of dealing with finicky moms and pops. On the other hand, if the opportunity is not legitimate, then you are their target number one. Either way, you have been selected to be on the guest list because you have more money than investment sense. The best advice is not to show up for this party

2. Don't compound your problems by investing with those who provide you with important financial services, such as your CPA or tax professional. Particularly tragic are those scams in which the victim lost money only to find themselves victimized a second time by tax fraud. The IRS is a formidable bill collector. Think they will make an allowance because you were victimized? Think again.

3. Never do business over the phone, Internet, or with anyone who comes knocking on your door. Of course, this doesn't apply to those with whom you have an established relationship, which doesn't include a friend of a friend you just met at a recent party or ballgame. You wouldn't buy a car from someone who approached you on the street, no matter what kind of bargain he or she offered. Why would you give money to someone who calls you on the phone or sends you an email? Once

again, make this a policy, and you'll have a much easier time turning these opportunities down.

4. Respect your investments. Don't mistreat them by using them as a way to impress your friends or as a way to feel "connected" or socially popular. You can bet that scammers are masters at converting your friendship into their income stream. Those with whom you invest are not your friends; they are your business partners. They may become your friends over time, once they have proven themselves. Keep a professional distance and you will have room to make rational, thoughtful decisions, free from the baggage of social pressure.

5. Let's face it, there is a short list of insiders who get the great deals. It's just the way of the world. Unless you happen to be a true insider, be doubly aware of these "insider" deals. Don't be flattered to be chosen from the teeming masses. If the deal were really that good, the big fish would have funded the entire enterprise themselves. When they don't, it means the risk is too great — even for them.

6. Don't be a sucker. Twelve percent a month interest, guaranteed. Double your money in a year. These would be laughable claims, if it weren't for the fact that so many have fallen for these pitches. One way to spot potential fraud is by the outrageousness of their claims. If banks are offering 1% annual interest, how could you friend Al, who works from an office in the back of a shopping center, have an investment that pays a 25% annual rate of return?

This is a harsh set of guidelines. It's meant to be that way. If you feel you must break any of these, at least limit your potential losses by accepting that you can, and most likely, will lose all of your investment. If you can live with that, have at it. However, for every missed opportunity to make money, you will have avoided dozens or more that will lose money. In the end, you will have to ask yourself if one score out of dozens makes up for all the others?

Where do you find legitimate investment opportunities? Like most people, from licensed professionals working for legitimate firms. These are trained investment professionals with something to lose when an investment fails. They are licensed security brokers, real estate brokers, and financial planners with a long list of accomplishments and credentials. They are respected members of the community and work for firms with a high profile. In fact, the company they work for might be more important than the individual, as these firms will have their own internal policing to root out bad-acting characters.

Have there been cases when investors have been defrauded even in the above instance? You bet. And that's why you need to access the reality of any investment regardless of who sponsors it

Past performance versus future outcomes

Past performance is not an indicator of future outcomes

This investment warning is repeated so often that no one gives it a second thought. Like a traffic sign along a well-traveled route, it seems to disappear into the investment landscape.

Over-familiarity, however, doesn't mean you should ignore the message. Consider these typical results from a recent study of mutual fund performance by Standard & Poor's: over the five year period ending September 2009, no large or mid-cap funds, and only one small-cap fund maintained a top-quartile ranking for the entire five years.

This study, along with many like it, shows clearly that chasing hot mutual funds is a losing game. Your cost of switching (combined with taxable gains) is a high price to pay for the seemingly random odds of finding the next high-performing fund. Staying on top of the investing game, even for the experts, is no easy task.

Practical investment advice

Want some investing suggestions free of chasing the next big thing? The next four sections provide a few well-proven avenues to maximize your investment returns, while minimizing your investment headaches.

Index funds

If you're at all familiar with investing, you've no doubt come across index funds. These are mutual funds containing the same stocks (in the same relative quantities) as popular stock indexes such as the S&P 500 (large companies) or the Russell 2000 (small companies). Instead of trying to consistently outperform any particular index, which has proven nearly impossible, even for the professionals, they only try to match its performance. The attraction of an index fund is the combination of consistent performance and low fees. For example, the Vanguard 500 Index fund, which invests in the largest 500 U.S. stocks, has outperformed over 80% of all U.S.-focused, actively managed stock mutual funds over the previous ten and twenty-five years ending June 30, 2013 (according to Morningstar Inc.). And, whereas a typical mutual fund charges annual fees of 1.32%, an index fund charges a mere fraction, only .17%. The largest index fund, Vanguard Total Stock Market Fund, charges a mere .06%.

With over 1,700 funds, tracking both stock and bond indexes, there is no end of options to diversify your investments. Some of the largest and most popular are the Vanguard 500, Fidelity Spartan 500, Vanguard Total Stock Market Index, and the Fidelity Spartan International Index.

ETFs or Exchange Traded Funds are yet another way to invest in an index. Because ETFs trade like stocks, you can do many of the same things as stocks, such as selling short, buying on margin, and even purchasing as little as one share. ETF expense ratios are also lower than those of the average mutual fund. However, when buying and selling ETFs, you have to pay the same commission to your broker that you'd pay on any regular stock order. Some of the most popular ETFs are ticker symbol SPY, which tracks the S&P 500 index; ticket symbol IVM, tracking the Russell 2000 index, and ticker symbol QQQ, tracking the NASDAQ 100 index.

Automatic investing

Often investors will combine investing in index funds with

automatic investing, which is a structured investment program that regularly transfers money from an investor's bank account into a pre-selected investment without any action on their part.

Investing a fixed amount on a regular schedule is also known as dollar cost averaging, because by default, an investor buys more when prices drop and less when they rise, thereby buying at an average between the highest and lowest prices, or the dollar cost average. For example, if you buy $1,000 of a given fund every month and the share price varies between $80 and $100, you will end up buying 12.5 shares when they are at their lowest prices and 10 shares when they are at their most expensive. Buying more at cheaper prices and less at more expensive prices is exactly what any investor would aspire to accomplish.

Automatic investing divorces your emotional mind from your investment decision making. You are forced to buy exactly when you feel that you shouldn't, which paradoxically is exactly when you should.

401(k)s and IRAs

401(k)s are tax-advantaged accounts established by your employer and funded through before-tax contributions from your paycheck. Within a 401(k) you typically are offered a number of investment options, all of which will grow tax-free until you begin to make withdrawals, whereupon you will pay taxes based upon your tax bracket at that time (typically lower than when you are working and making contributions). If you make withdrawals before age 59½ you will have to pay a penalty. Often, employers will match employee contributions of up to 6% of the employee's salary. In addition, should you have a financial emergency, you can always borrow money from your 401(k), provided you pay it all back in the future.

IRAs are set up by individuals and provide the same tax benefits as 401(k)s and include the same withdrawal restrictions. IRAs can be either traditional or Roth IRAs. The latter offers tax-deductible contributions and taxable withdrawals, while the former doesn't offer tax-free contributions, but instead provides tax-free withdrawals. For those who expect to grow their IRA to a substantial size, tax-free withdrawals are a significant plus.

Annuities

An annuity is most often an insurance product that pays an income based upon making an upfront investment. Annuities are a popular choice for those who want to receive a steady income stream in retirement, free of the hassles of actively managing their own investments.

Annuities offload those investment decisions onto an insurance company, which in turn provides investors with a guaranteed income. Of course, as you know from reading the section on risk, such guarantees come at a price. Instead of directly assuming the risk and reward of their investments, annuity investors have essentially transferred the risks and rewards to an insurance company. For the privilege of receiving a predictable income, they also give up some of the returns that they might have enjoyed had they invested on their own. Additionally, they also inherit the risk that the insurance company might fail. While unthinkable only a few years ago, the last recession proved that every financial institution has the potential to fail.

The income you receive from an annuity can be paid to you monthly, quarterly, annually, or even in a lump sum payment. You can opt to receive payments for the rest of your life, or for a set number of years. You can also opt for a guaranteed payout (fixed annuity) or a payout stream determined by the performance of your annuity's underlying investments (variable annuity).

There are two basic types of annuities: deferred and immediate. With a deferred annuity, your money is invested for a period of time until you are ready to begin taking withdrawals, usually coinciding with retirement. If you opt for an immediate annuity, you begin to receive payments soon after you make your initial investment. Deferred and immediate annuities can also be of either the fixed or variable type.

Money invested in annuities grows tax-free until withdrawn, just like Roth IRAs. Unlike IRAs, however, there is no contribution limit.

Annuities often carry hefty charges, including sizable sales commissions as high as 10%, surrender charges if you should decide to withdraw any of your annuity investment, and management fees above the average for actively managed mutual funds. However, low-cost annuity alternatives, offered by non-insurance companies such as Fidelity, Schwab, Vanguard, T. Rowe Price and TIAA-CREF, are beginning to make their appearance.

Many investors include some annuity products in their retirement portfolio. Whether these make sense for you depends upon how well you can manage your own investments. If you have the time and the inclination, you will probably come out money ahead by managing your own well-diversified investment portfolio, combined with a disciplined withdrawal strategy, such as the MRMD approach mentioned in a previous chapter. If you would rather dispense with those hassles, annuities might work for you provided you shop for the best products — those with the lowest fees and the strongest sponsors.

Summary

In the end, successful investing is all about self-discipline — overcoming your fears when buying opportunities emerge, while avoiding the temptation to turn aggressive just when caution would win the day. If these tendencies drive your investment decisions, then you are best advised to establish structured investment plans, such as automatic investing in index funds, so that you won't be tempted to do the wrong thing at the wrong time.

A long-term focus in conjunction with a regular program of investing will ultimately yield the best, long-term results. Don't turn investing into a casino game. It isn't about playing the odds. Nor is it about swinging for the fences with some wild investment opportunity cooked up by your neighbor. It's about making a rational plan and seeing it through, in both good times and bad.

Final Thoughts

Congratulations. The time you've spent reading this book is an investment in a better future for yourself and your family. Personal finance is fundamentally about knowing what to do and when to do it — something you have now learned. It's a mistake to think that effectively managing your finances requires some specialized degree in business or finance; no more than managing your health means you need a degree in medicine.

What you need is a grasp of the basic principles accompanied by the right temperament. Successful financial temperament comes from first recognizing your mental biases, then developing ways to avoid them. Snap decisions, fear of loss avoidance, regret, and so on are the stuff of everyday life. You must see these for what they are — wealth destroyers. When you put off retirement planning, jump into sketchy investments, or put too much faith in your own abilities, you are only robbing yourself of your future.

If you lack the temperament or interest to manage your own money, then you should set up structured programs to compensate, like those we've covered Chapters 10 and 11. What you mustn't do, like so many, is to delegate your financial responsibility to someone else. No one cares about your money as much as you do, including brokers, advisors, and bankers. They care about themselves first, meaning you have a built-in conflict of interest from the start.

This doesn't mean you shouldn't use financial advisors, only that you must manage them. It's akin to telling an architect that you want him to design a nice house and then turning him loose from there on out. If you want that nice house, you have to learn to work with him, learn something about architecture, and stay engaged as the project commences. Your personal finances are no different.

Effective money management doesn't mean you have to master every financial skill either. Just as with building a house, you don't have to nail together the framing, nor put on the roof. You can, but it's certainly not required. Similarly, with your finances, you don't have to clip coupons, pick individual stocks, and master the intricacies of financial statements. You only have to know enough to manage those who you want to do it for you.

Jumping on the latest financial trends is rarely profitable. Personal finance is not that complicated in the first place. For most people, what you have learned from this book is sufficient to see you through your entire life, provided that you apply it. Knowledge not applied is no better than ignorance, worse perhaps, because then you have no excuses.

If you integrate your new-found financial knowledge into your everyday thinking, you will discover just how little it takes to manage your money. You don't need to put yourself on a severe financial diet, downsize your house, or live in your car. In fact, do as little as possible, except when necessary. In the long run, this approach will provide the best balance between building wealth and living a fulfilling life.

Appendix A   Compound Interest

You cannot hope to successfully manage your money without understanding compound interest. It lies at the very heart of lending, savings, retirement planning, and investing. Without it, modern finance would not exist. It can be a powerful wealth builder, or used unwisely, a wealth destroyer.

Let's begin with some basics drawn from the world of lending. This is where most people get their first education in compound interest. As you already know, banks and other lenders make loans in order to earn interest, which is a charge the borrower pays to the lender for the use of the lender's money.

The money on which you pay interest is called the principal.

Loan interest charges are calculated by multiplying the loan principal by the loan interest rate. This rate is stated as some percentage for a given amount of time, such as 1% per month or 12% per year. If for example, you were to borrow $100 for one month at an interest rate of 1% per month then you would owe $100 x .01 = $1.00 of interest at the end of one month. Seems pretty easy so far. However, what happens at the end of the second month? Now there are two ways to calculate this. One way is to again charge 1% interest on the original $100 for the second month, which again equals $1.00. This is called simple interest, meaning that the interest rate is always applied against the original loan principal. If you were to borrow the $100 for 5 months, then each month's interest charge of $1.00 would be added together for five months to arrive at a total of $5.00.

The mathematical formula is as follows:

Simple Interest Charges = Principal x Interest rate x
Number of periods

In our example, the loan principal is $100 and the monthly interest rate is 1%. The simple interest due after five months would be calculated as follows:

$100 principal x 1% interest rate x 5 months = $5.00

The second way to calculate interest charges is called compound interest. Although the difference may appear to be subtle, the ultimate effect is not. Using the same example, recall that at the end of the first month, the interest charge on the original $100 principal was $1.00. For the second month, the principal is increased by the $1.00 interest charge bringing the total principal to $101.00. Then the interest rate of 1% per month is applied to this new principal amount. The result is as follows:

Table A-1

Month 1:	$100 principal x .01 interest rate = $1.00 interest
Month 2:	$100 principal + $1.00 interest from previous month = $101 principal x .01 interest rate = $1.01 interest
Total Interest	$1.00 + $1.01 = $2.01

Instead of owing $2.00 using simple interest, the borrower instead owes $2.01. This is the compounding part of compound interest. The interest charges from one month are added onto the principal balance from the previous month and so on until the principal is repaid.

Looking at a 5-month example, the total outstanding interest charges are as follows:

Table A-2

Month 1: $100 x .01   = $1.00
Month 2: ($100 + $1.00) x 01   = $1.01
Month 3: ($100 + $1.00 + $1.01) x .01   = $1.02
Month 4: ($100 + $1.00 + $1.01 + 1.02) x .01   = $1.03
Month 5: ($100 + $1.00 + $1.01 + 1.02 + 1.03) x .01 = $1.04

Total $5.10

The difference between $5.00 and $5.10 may not seem like much, but compound interest builds like a locomotive. When it leaves the station, it moves very slowly, but after a period of time it can take out anything in its path. Using the above example, let's see what happens to the total outstanding principal after 50 years (600 months), once again comparing simple and compound interest rates.

Simple Interest Charges

Total interest charge due after 50 years =
$100 principal x 1% interest x 600 months = **$600.00**

Compound Interest Charges

Total interest charge due after 50 years =
$((1 + .01)^{600})$ interest x $100 principal) = **$39,158.34**

Don't worry if you can't follow the calculations for compound interest as they can get complicated when expressed in a mathematical formula. However, do note the difference in the totals. With compound interest, that extra one cent per month at the beginning ends up making a difference of $38,558.34 in the end! This gives you an idea of how credit card balances can get so out of control when the borrower makes only minimum payments.

Annual percentage rate

Typically, when lenders express interest charges they will use a one-year time period. This *annual percentage rate,* or APR, is a way to state interest charges in a way that standardizes them. So instead of one lender stating that their interest charge is 2% per every 17 days and another stating that theirs is 5% per every 3 months, they all use a one-year, or annual, period.

However, this standardized annual rate may still differ depending upon whether the lender chooses to use simple or compound interest, as the following two examples will show. Both use the same interest rate of 1% per month.

$$\text{Simple annual interest rate} = 1\% \text{ monthly rate x } 12 = 12\% \text{ APR}$$

$$\text{Compound annual interest rate} = (1\% \text{ monthly rate})^{12} = 12.68\% \text{ APR}$$

As you can see, two loans may have the same 1% per month interest rate, but the one that uses compounding will always have a greater APR than the one using simple interest. Lenders are required to show the APR for their loans so that borrowers can make comparisons between lenders based upon the annual cost of borrowing. Be forewarned, for some loans, lenders can choose to advertise either simple interest or compound interest. And, as you now know, simple interest can substantially understate the true cost of borrowing.

In addition, lenders must also include any loan fees or other loan-related expenses in the APR calculation. For example, a $100 loan with a 1% monthly rate of interest (using compound interest) without any fees has a 12.68% APR as shown earlier, while the same loan with a $10 fee upfront would have a first year APR of 22.68%. The loan fee is treated the same as if it were an additional interest charge paid in the first year.

Let's look at how compound interest affects your credit card debt. As you know, if you do not pay the amount you owe on your card within the grace period, you then have to make at least a minimum payment every month.

Because credit cards rely only on your promise to pay off your debt, the interest charges are generally quite high. How much higher? Let's say you have a $100 balance on your card and you plan to pay it off in equal payments of $10 per month. With interest charges included, instead of 10 months ($10 per month times 10 months = $100), it will actually take 11 months. So you wind up paying a total of $110 in order to pay off your original $100 balance.

Paying an extra $10 over a year's time for the privilege of having $100 to spend right away may not sound like such a bad deal. However, watch what happens when the balance is $1,000, but you still only pay $10 per month.

If you make monthly payments of $10 on a credit card balance of $1,000, you will never pay it off, no matter how many payments you make.
Ever.

Shocked? How can this be? Because the interest charges on the $1,000 are equal to your monthly payment. Even if you double your monthly payment to $20 per month, it will still take you approximately six years to pay it off in full. In the end, you will pay $400 in interest charges or a third more than the total amount of money you borrowed in the first place. That $1,000 will cost you $1,400 when it's all said and done. Still sound like a great deal?

Credit card debt is one of the fastest ways to get into trouble. Credit card companies are happy to let you keep borrowing because the interest charges add up so rapidly, especially if you make small monthly payments.

Compound interest and savings accounts

Now, consider what would have happened if you had deposited the $100 from the above example into your savings, instead of borrowing it. Let's say you invested it for 20 years at 1% per month interest or 12.68% APR. At the end of that time, you would have had over 10 times more than your initial deposit, or a total of $1,089.25. In essence, you have switched places with the bank, and they now pay you interest for keeping your money in savings. Of course, 12.68% APR is a very high interest rate, which banks don't pay for savings; however, the power of compounding is still a powerful force even with interest rates of 3, 4, or 5%, providing you leave the money alone for a long enough period of time.

Taxes

If you invest your money in a savings account or any
investment that offers a compound interest return, even
a dividend paying stock, then you have to take taxes into
account. Look at the following example. In the first instance,
$1,000 is deposited into a tax-free account paying 3% per
year and in the second, the same amount is deposited into a
nontaxable account paying the same 3% per year. Assume also
that you are in the 25% tax bracket, meaning you pay 25% of
you interest income in taxes.

Table A-3

	Taxable Account	Non Taxable Account	Difference
Initial Deposit	$1,000	$1,000	
5 years	$1,118	$1,162	$44
10 years	$1,252	$1,349	$97
20 years	$1,567	$1,820	$253

As you can see, the nontaxable account ends up with nearly
16% more. Generally, the best advice is that any investment
which depends upon compounding returns is best invested in
a nontaxable account.

Rule of 72

A very helpful mental shortcut for calculating compound
interest is called the rule of 72. In essence, if you divide 72 by
the annual interest rate, the result will be the number of years
required for your investment to double in value. For example,

if you take the above case of $1,000 invested in a nontaxable account at 3%, the result of dividing 72 by 3 equals 24. It will take 24 years for your investment to double in value.

Now, what if you had invested the same $1,000 in a taxable account? Simple. You first reduce your expected rate of interest by your tax rate. In this case, you are in the 25% tax bracket, so reducing 3% interest rate by 25% gives you 2.25%. Now you can divide 72 by 2.25% and you will get an answer of 32 years, which means it will take your investment 8 more years to double in value.

Summary

Compound interest lies at the heart of money management. Used wisely, it can build your wealth steadily for your entire life. Before you take on any significant debt, take the time to calculate the true cost of paying it all back. Always remember, those interest expenses come out of your future earnings, which could be in your pocket, instead of the bank's.

About the Authors

Wes Karchut has over twenty five years of experience in business and finance. In addition to holding numerous senior-level management positions, he was a principal in a private equity technology fund. He received his M.B.A. in Finance from the University of Wisconsin, Madison.

Darby Karchut has taught social studies at a nationally recognized junior high school for over fifteen years. She has received numerous educational awards — most recently a commendation from her school district for her contribution to teen literacy. She earned her M.Ed. from The Colorado College.

Bibliography

Besiger, Gegory. *Personal finance for People Who Hate Personal Finance*. Liam Judge Pub., 2010. eBook

Coleman, Aaron. *Winning with Money: The Budget Tool for People Who Hate Budgets*. Russell Media, 2011. eBook

"Direct Satafford Loans." Student Aid. n.d. Web. 30 June 2012

"FHA Requirements: Debt Guidelines." *FHA Requirements*. FHA n.d. Web 6 June 2012

Garment, Thomas and Fogue, Raymond. *Personal Finance*. Ohio: South-Western College Pub., 2009. Print.

Holden, Lewis. "A Check Is a Check: Whatever It's Printed On." *Blogs* Bankrate n.d. Web 6 June 2012.

Kessel, Brent. *It's Not About the Money: Unlock Your Money Type to Achieve Spiritual and Financial Abundance*. New York: Harper Collins, 2008. Print.

Koblinger, Beth. *Get a Financial Life: Personal Finance in Your Twenties and Thirties*. New York: Simon and Schuster, Inc., 2009. Print

Stanley, Thomas and Danko, William. *The Millionaire Next Door*. Simon and Schuster, Inc., 1996. Print

Statman, Meir. *The Mistakes We Make and Why We Make Them*. Wall Street Journal, 2009. Web 28 August 2013

Burica, Barbara and Iams,Howard, et. al. *The Disappearing Defined Benefit Pension and Its Potential Impact on the Retirement Incomes of Baby Boomers*. Social Security Bulletin, Vol. 69. No. 3, 2009 Web 15, Aug 2013

Index

A

adjustable rate loans, 118
anchoring, 20
ATM cards, 56
automatic payment, 60, 178

B

balance sheet, 86
  current liabilities, 80
  large assets, 80
  liabilities, 80
  liquid assets, 79
  long-term liabilities, 80
balloon loans 116
balloon payment, 116
behavioral economics, 150
behavioral finance, 150
billing errors, 53
branding, 21
bundling, 20

C

CARD Act in 2009, 57
CLEM expenses, 42
collegemeasures.org, 92
commodity, 17
compound interest, 186
credit cards
  consumer protections 52
  grace period, 51
credit score
  component, 70, 72
credit reporting agencies, 66
current liabilities, 80

D

debit cards, 50
  1975 Fair Credit Billing Act, 52
  debit card hold, 56

L

M

N

O

P

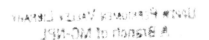